MILK
FOR
BABES

MILK
FOR
BABES

Using the Bible to Find the
Answers to Life's Questions

Anne Ferrell
Murchison

WORD BOOKS
PUBLISHER
WACO, TEXAS

All Scripture quotations, unless otherwise noted, are from *The
Living Bible, Paraphrased* (Wheaton: Tyndale House Publishers,
copyright 1971) and are used by permission.
Scripture quotations marked *Amplified* are from *The Amplified
Bible*, copyright © 1965 by Zondervan Publishing House;
those marked NIV are from The Holy Bible, New International
Version, copyright © 1978 by New York International Bible Society.

ISBN 0–8499–2868–0
Library of Congress catalog card number: 78–63745
Printed in the United States of America

Grateful acknowledgment is made to the following: Fleming H. Revell
Co., for permission to paraphrase a brief statement from *Maximum
Marriage* by Tim Timmons; Harcourt Brace Jovanich, Inc., for
permission to paraphrase a brief statement from *Surprised by Joy*
by C. S. Lewis (1966); Tyndale House Publishers for permission
to use as a statement the title *Christianity Is Jewish* by Edith
Schaeffer; Crossroads Publications for permission to use a
quotation from *America: Garden of the Gods* by James Robison as
a chapter title.

First Printing, July 1979
Second Printing, November 1979
Third Printing, February 1980

This book is dedicated first and foremost to the glory of God, the Father, Son and Holy Spirit
and
To my husband, Clint, and my children, Frank and Wendy, who have my deepest love and gratitude for their love and encouragement and for the comfort of their company in the Kingdom of God.

Acknowledgments

THE MOST IMPORTANT thank-you of all belongs to the Lord, who, through his Holy Spirit, enabled me to write this book, but the second most important thank-you belongs to the Body of Christ (God's children), without whose prayers through these months of writing and speaking I could not have gotten it all done. To them, a big thank-you and God-bless.

There are so many people in my life for whom I am thankful. A special note of appreciation to Josephine Campbell, Amy and French Jones, Lucia DeBose, Janis Coffee, Dottie Dowe, Ann Rosenberg, and my husband Clint for their input and loving guidance on this book. An extra-special thank-you goes to Janis Coffee, who introduced me to Jesus Christ and lovingly and patiently nurtured me with unconditional love and a generous portion of God's Word the first year of "infancy" in him.

Also, my deepest gratitude to Tom Landry for his interest and help at a most difficult time of year for him.

This list could go on and on. So many of God's children have "fed" me spiritually over these early years in my Christian walk that it is impossible for me to separate the flow of teachings I have had from my own thoughts. We haven't agreed on everything, and I thank God that we haven't *had* to, but so much of each one of them is a part of me and, therefore, a part of this book.

Last, but by no means least!! The beautiful people who work for me and have kept my house running smoothly so that I have had the time and serenity to work these endless

hours deserve and are given a great deal of the credit . . .
and it is *richly* deserved, because I have not only had their
complete cooperation, but their prayers, encouragement,
and enthusiasm as well. And for the "last but not least," this
beautiful promise of God . . .

Luke 13:30: "And, behold, there are last which shall be first,
   and there are first which shall be last" (KJV).

Contents

Foreword

1 Peter 2:2: "As newborn babes, desire the sincere milk of the Word, that ye may grow thereby."

WHEN ANNE became a Christian several years ago, she would from time to time enthusiastically share a belief which, in turn, would elicit from me a question. My questions were of a very simple nature; so simple, in fact, that the answers to them are generally passed over or assumed in more advanced books on Christianity.

Milk for Babes consists of those very questions and answers, and the answers which she gave me were not interpretations of the Scriptures—they *were* the Scriptures, both from the Old and New Testaments.

What Anne has written is a book for novices like me, and at its very heart is an idea so simple that almost nobody expresses it: that is, that to gain eternal life in Heaven it is *only* necessary to accept Jesus Christ as Lord and Savior. That is a rich serving of milk, but expressed in a way that even a babe like me can understand it.

Clint Murchison, Jr.

Preface

ANNE MURCHISON WAS inspired to write this book out of her love for God and his love for her. She has revealed her life to you as a witness to the power of God's love and his grace. I can share her enthusiasm since I have received the same gift from God through his Son, Jesus Christ—a gift that is shared by millions of believers throughout the world.

She has made clear the full meaning of the Gospel, so that new believers may have a better understanding of God's plan of salvation. To the nonbeliever, her prayer is that the Holy Spirit will challenge you to live "a more excellent way."

It took me many years of trying to "climb the ladder of success" before I made the great discovery that the purpose of life is to find the right relationship with God, our creator. My discovery came because a friend cared enough for me to encourage me to study the Bible.

Human nature makes us skeptical of many things and the Bible is no exception. The Bible says, "For it is by faith that we are saved," not by works or human reasoning. When the so-called religious leaders of Jesus' time confronted him and asked him for a "sign," Jesus replied, "If you will follow my teachings, then you will know whether I am from God or man."

Many people in our society today believe that Christianity, or religion, is a sign of weakness—"an opium for the people." The only reason they feel that way is they have never "taken up their cross and followed Jesus." To stand among your friends, peers, or business associates and live a

Christian life takes more courage and conviction than you would ever need to win a Super Bowl or reach the top of your social or business circle.

Whether you are a believer or nonbeliever in Jesus Christ, the challenge of Christianity brings up questions that need answering. Anne Murchison has used these questions as topics for her study guide. She has allowed the Word of God, *the Bible*, to answer these questions.

The doubts we all have from time to time, whether we are believers or nonbelievers, are not necessarily bad.

Robert Browning wrote a poem:

> You call for faith, I give you doubt to
>   prove that faith exists,
> The greater the doubt, the stronger the
>   faith, I say
> If faith overcomes doubt.

The challenge of this book is that your faith may become strong and steady so that you may be able to fully enjoy "the abundant life" Jesus promised.

For those of you who are new believers, I encourage you to use this book as a study guide for your time in the Bible. The Holy Spirit will reveal to you only what you are able to handle. As you continue to grow and mature as a Christian, God will continue to reveal new truths that will enable you to fully enjoy the "peace that passes all understanding."

May God bless you,

Tom Landry

God uses his Word
to
pierce the heart of man

"Money may buy the husk of many things, but not the kernel. It brings you food but not appetite, medicine but not health, acquaintances but not friends, servants but not faithfulness, days of joy but not peace and happiness."
—Henrik Ibsen

"I'm glad that He has given me much more than wealth or fame, for He's called me by His name, and that's why I proclaim the message of His grace through His music." *
—Chuck Gagliardi

"I am come that they might have life, and that they might have it more abundantly."—Jesus Christ

My Story

ONE YEAR and a half after I became a Christian, my husband and I were entertaining some business associates and their wives at a football game at Texas Stadium and later they stopped by our home.

As the men were discussing their business deals, the wives and I took a tour of our home. In our dining room, there is an abstract portrait of me which was done by a fine artist and dear friend—a work of art I have always loved and admired. One of the women in the group made a startling observation. "I like the painting very much," she said. "And I know it's your portrait, but there is a sad quality about the woman in the painting that I definitely don't see in the you standing before me." This woman knew nothing about me!

Her statement caught me somewhat off-guard. Until that very moment I had not realized that the drastic change which had been taking place inside over the previous year and a half was so visible on the outside.

The following is my story.

I spent the first thirty-five years of my life searching for answers to questions that plague us all through our lives . . . "Why was I born?" . . . "Why am I living?" . . . "Is that all there is?" . . . "What's it all about?" I believe these questions plague most of us, because there have been so many songs written about them—songs in every generation about the futility, vanity, and emptiness of life. But as is the case with most people, I was looking for the answers in all the wrong places. Today I can honestly say that my searching is over. I have discovered the only answer that could end that search. Today I am freer to accept life as it is and to grow with my circumstances than I have ever been before.

I read somewhere that what happens to us is not important. How we react to it is! Life is a grindstone, and whether it grinds us down or polishes us up depends on the stuff of which we are made. I believe that Christ is the pumice we can add to our beings to create the polish. That's why I'm so delighted to share the wonder and beauty of The Pumice with you, because for the first thirty-five years of my being, life was not only grinding me down but chewing me up!

I had been a Christian for two years before I was able to admit to others that I had been hiding behind a mask all of my life—a mask that said, "I am strong . . . I can handle anything . . . I am okay." Only then could I bare my deepest self—the real me . . . the frightened child . . . the little girl who, all my life, went into a closet to cry because I felt so isolated and alone. Crying, for me, was not merely shedding a few tears every now and then. Rather, crying was an almost daily time when I sobbed heart-brokenly for hours, in a world of isolation and aloneness that was unbearable. Yet I was busy . . . well thought-of . . . and surrounded by people!

Behind my mask of confidence and self-assurance lurked abject despair about my life. Hardly a day passed that I did not pray to a God I was not even sure was there to *please* let me die. Life was unbearable for me and I so wanted to give up. My mask was so impenetrable that even my husbands and best friends could not see this part of me. I had become very accomplished at living the lie that was my life.

Today, I still appear to be a person who "has it all together," but I'd like to admit to you right now that I do not . . . and I never will. All my life, I reached for the impossible dream of getting it all together. Now I am free to accept the fact that there are always going to be times in my life when I won't! Why am I free to accept this? Well, I have discovered through studying the godly men of the Bible—David, Paul, Jeremiah, Isaiah, to name just a few—that they never did get it all together either. But, like David, Paul, Jeremiah, Isaiah and the others, I do have an incredible calmness and serenity beneath me that cannot be shaken under any circumstances. Though I sometimes bog down beneath the weight of day-to-day living, I can usually pinpoint at those times that I have quit trusting in the Lord and gotten back into relying on myself. It's precious of him, though, that without fail, as soon as I am ready to put my trust and reliance back in him the foundation beneath my feet is more solid than ever! Not with an "I-told-you-so" kind of feeling, but with love and warmth . . . a "welcome-back . . . I've-missed-you-and-I'm-so-glad-you've-returned" kind of feeling. It's at times such as these that I realize the foundation was always there just waiting for me to place my feet back upon it.

I could say of my past that I ran through life . . . taking what I wanted . . . doing what I wanted . . . and when I got what I "wanted" . . . whatever that might have been . . . that I settled down to the good life and the "goody-goody" life of a super Christian. I would like to admit that I did go through life seeking what I wanted, and never finding it; doing what I wanted (when my job and children allowed it), and never finding it satisfying. What I hope you hear through my story is that Jesus Christ is in the business of changing lives; that I don't have all the answers, but that *he* does. Life hasn't suddenly become perfect, and neither have I. But after years of endless and restless searching, I have finally found a resting place. Knowing that Jesus Christ died for me just the way I am and that

he cherishes me—Anne Murchison—that's the only answer
I really need! It has given me hope and freedom . . . hope
for a better life and freedom from guilt . . . freedom to a
big extent from myself.

My life has so much joy and peace now. One of the
reasons I am so thrilled is that I hurt so badly for so long
that when I finally stopped hurting I felt so good! The
longer I feel good, the more I feel good. The longer I walk
with Jesus Christ, the more light I have and the more light
I have, the less the darkness can exist . . . and the more
light I have, the more dramatic the contrast with the darkness of my old life. I didn't really know how dark it was until
the light began to shine. Psalm 18:28 says, "For thou wilt
light my lamp; the Lord, my God, will lighten my darkness."

The circumstances of my life are interesting, but through
them I hope to share something even more interesting. I've
learned that circumstances are a special gift from God,
and that he uses those circumstances in a fascinating and
important way to weave the fabric of our lives. That's right!
Even our ostensibly rotten circumstances are a *gift* from
God. Our circumstances are the avenues God uses in each
of our lives to woo us . . . to draw us to him. (I don't mean
to imply that God *causes* rotten circumstances, because he
isn't the one who does that! We are! But he takes the rotten
circumstances and uses them in such a beautiful way in our
lives that they become gifts.)

I grew up in a very distressed home. My mother is a
recovering alcoholic, but those years when I was living at
home were pure torment for us all, because she was still
drinking. Alcoholism is not a sickness of *one* person in a
family. Alcoholism is a family sickness that involves every
member of the family, and it is tragic that that sickness is
one of our nation's—world's—leading killers. But this is my
background. I thank God that my mother has been sober
now for nine years. I thank God that we are all recovering
from the sickness of alcohol.

As a family, we attended church on a regular basis, but
not one of us knew Jesus Christ personally. Not one of us
knew why we attended church, except that it was the "right
thing to do." It was the "proper way to raise children."

For years I grieved over my painful childhood. But in Joel 2:25 God promises that he will "restore the years the locusts have eaten" in our lives. Now that Jesus Christ is my Lord, I am able to see him doing just that in my life, my husband's life, and in the lives of my children, who are badly scarred by a multi-divorced mother who worked too hard and played too hard.

Yes, as we make our inevitable mistakes with our lives and with the lives of those around us, God is just waiting to heal the hurts. All we have to do is claim his promises for ourselves and *believe* them. By believing that God can redeem the lost years and claiming that promise from God, I am victorious. He is not only restoring those years but he is showing me how he handpicked my life for me. He knows where I need to grow and what it will take to accomplish that in me. He handpicked my pains and joys, my poverty and my wealth . . . (and I'd like you to know that I *have* experienced poverty . . . I *have* had to worry about where the next meal was coming from. I *know* what that is like).

In his book *Maximum Marriage*, Tim Timmons says that if we do not accept lovingly the faults of our spouse, we are rejecting a gift from God, because God handpicked our spouse with the perfect strengths and weaknesses for us, in order that we might grow in the areas of our own weaknesses.

I believe this is also true of our parents. I look back in shame at how much I rejected God's gifts of pain and suffering and the growth he intended for me. But, he never lets us escape that growth; it always catches up with us sooner or later. If it doesn't, we never find that peace and joy we are inherently seeking.

When we run from God's plans for us, we must face our growth areas with someone else. I see it as taking "detours" from the main road of life. Every "detour" (that is, deliberate act of my own will—saying "no" to God's plan) ultimately leads me back to the main road (God's perfect plan for my life, which involves maturing me where only he knows I need it and thereby deepening my faith in him, slowly conforming me to his image, and bringing me into a closer, more intimate relationship with him, because that's really why he created us—to fellowship with him, to love and worship him!). Jeremiah 29:11 says, "For I know the plans I have for you, says the Lord. They are plans for good and not for evil, to give you a future and a hope."

And, so the progression began in my life—the first in a long series of "detours." Hoping to escape from my unhappiness at home, I married and at seventeen had my first baby. The boy I married was exactly that—a boy. And I was a girl. Two children expecting a baby. We were so young and so frightened. Our first child, a little boy, was born in November, and in January my husband went overseas for eighteen months. During that time, I found myself back at home with my parents, but now with a baby of my own. That's right . . . God gave me another chance to accept his plans for my growth with my parents, but I still said "no" to him.

At the same time I was trying to finish high school and take care of a baby, I received no communication at all from my husband—not a letter, a Christmas card, a birthday card nor a telephone call. It was truly the loneliest, most anguishing eighteen months of my life. But at the end of his tour of duty in Okinawa, he returned. He never gave me an explanation for his silence of eighteen months, but I know that it was a time that was just as bleak and lonely for him as it was for me. So we picked up our lives and started over, and a year later we had a baby girl too. Then after two years, along came another detour for me; I said "no" to God for the second time, and that marriage ended in divorce.

At age twenty, I found myself divorced and responsible for two young children and still running from God's plans for my life. Within six months, out of fear and insecurity, I remarried; three months later I said "no" to God again and was divorced again . . . and still running. The second marriage did bring me to Dallas, and Dallas has been home to me ever since. From 22 to 29, a long seven years, I remained single, supporting my two children by working as a legal secretary, often for as many as sixty hours a week. I also played very hard. In fact, I could say that I lived on the wild side of life for a number of years. Running . . .

running . . . running. And saying "no" to God every minute
of every day. My detours got longer and longer.

In 1970, I married again, and for the third time, I married
for the wrong reason. I continued to look to people to make
me happy . . . to change my life . . . and that never does
work for very long. After four years, I said "no" to God
again. I did not yet know that God could turn my wrongs
into his rights, that he was the only One who could change
my life or end the searching. In fact, I didn't even care to
know. But . . . do you think God loved me any less? Do
you think he gave up on me? I can assure you that *he did
not!* In fact, he pursued me with even more intensity. God's
pursuit is relentless.

In 1975, I married for the fourth time. But I thought this
time was different. This was the "love of my life." This was
not a desperation move. This was where I had always
wanted to be.

I can almost hear the wheels grinding as you are reading
this. You may be thinking, "Sure. Who wouldn't want to
have all that *she* has?" As Satan said to God about Job,
"Haven't you made a hedge about him and about his house
and about all that he has on every side?" In other words,
why shouldn't Job be a godly man? He had everything any
man could ever want. But God knew that what Job really
had was something far more precious than any earthly
treasure and that was a deep, personal relationship with
God that surpassed by far anything Job might physically
possess.

I have now learned through the tender and merciful love
and guidance of the Lord that our earthly appetites can
never be satisfied by anything or anyone but Jesus Christ.
In fact, I sought all my answers from the world, and the
world gave me every answer it had to give me . . . those
things most of us think will make us happy (or at least hap-
pier)! Those answers did not and could not fill the void
in me. In fact, the void grew larger and larger. Then the
Lord revealed that void in me in all its fullness and at the
same time he showed me how to fill it.

In the midst of my most abject depression, he brought
me to hear the Christian testimony of a dear, precious

friend, Janis Coffee, at Christian Women's Club in Dallas.
I say he brought me, because I learned over a year later
that Janis had been praying with friends about whether or
not to ask me. She is not exactly the kind of person who
would walk up and say, "I'm speaking to a group of women
next week. Would you like to come?" But God answered
her prayers. His answer was a loud, resounding "YES." One
night at a political black-tie dinner party, God literally
dropped me in her lap! There I sat at the table across from
her. The Lord gave her a gentle nudge and said, "There
she is. Go ahead and ask her." She did and I did and her
story touched me at the very core of my being. I was
brought into the everlasting arms of Jesus Christ that day—
February 12, 1976. I finally faced the fact that "my way"
had never worked. "My way" had been the way of disaster.
I simply said, "I give up. I've made such a mess out of my
life and the lives of those around me that I am finally willing to try it your way." At that moment I experienced a
profound sense of relief. It was unmistakably the peace of
God. For me it was a similar experience to pregnancy.
When a child is conceived within the mother's womb, it is
microscopic in size, no larger than a germ. Yet each day
that seed grows larger and larger. Every mother who has
carried a child has lived with this sense of carrying a real
person around with her twenty-four hours a day, and there
is a real sense of "loss" when the baby is born . . . when
it is no longer comfortably with the mother all the time.
This is where the similarity ends. Childbirth is a joyful experience and wonderful and new things proceed from
there, but that close bond of flesh within flesh is gone. When
Jesus Christ came to live in my heart, he felt no larger than
a germ—a seed—but with every passing day his presence
within me grows, and that is a presence I will *never* have to
part with. Hebrews 13:5 promises, ". . . I will never, never
fail you nor forsake you." Thus, the lonely void in my life
began to fill the moment I invited him into my life.

My visible life really does appear to be everything little
girls dream of—marrying Prince Charming—though as an
aside, Clint Murchison is better known for owning the
Dallas Cowboys than he is for being a Prince Charming.

But at the time of our marriage I believed he really was Prince Charming; in fact, he was my god.

Clint is quiet and painfully shy, and there are many wonderful, sweet qualities he tries very hard to conceal. He is a brilliant and multi-talented man, a rare combination of scientist, artist, and astute businessman. He is a prankster, a clown and a tease. Until a few years ago, these were the ways he communicated to people best. But more and more he is learning to share on a new level. He is a witty, tender husband and friend, and God is changing him . . . he is becoming a prince.

We have our own private island in the Bahamas, a beautiful penthouse in New York and an absolutely gorgeous home in Dallas, Texas, right in the middle of twenty-five acres of perfectly manicured grounds, all staffed with lots and lots of servants. There are a number of airplanes to take me anywhere I might wish, on the most exotic trips, with VIP treatment wherever we go. I have a closet full of the finest clothes. If I choose to, I would never have to lift a finger. But for me there truly was an emptiness to all of these "delicious" luxuries, and my realized fantasies did not bring me happiness. I got more and more depressed with each day.

There are no fairy-tale lives. In addition to the adjustments of being newly married, there were lots of other adjustments to be made, and, since I had never known who I really was, the added pressure of my new-found and very public status brought on a real identity crisis. Ultimately this worked for my good, because it forced me to begin to try to find out who I was and what was really expected of me. There were lots of pressures and stresses I never dreamed I would have to deal with, and anxiety and depression were my constant companions.

For two years, I was in therapy with a wonderful man who walked hand in hand with me through the darkest of times. He helped me see that all my life I had been hitting myself and others over the head with my guilt, my failures, my self-pity, and my despair. I believe that there are no accidents with God, and that he sent me this man, this friend, to help me sort through the guilt of my life—the guilt that haunted me in the dark hours of the endless nights of my life.

One of the most powerful things that drew me to Jesus Christ was the realization that in spite of my mistakes, God never stopped loving me, nor did his love waver in the least. I finally found a place to put those failures, guilts, and despairs, and that place was in the very big hands of Jesus Christ, who had been waiting for me to do that all my life. God's unconditional love and forgiveness is what saved me and what is healing me more every day I walk with him. I finally said "yes" to God, and saying "yes" to God has given me the freedom to be me.

I truly believed I could live happily ever after! I see now, though, that God allowed me to gain everything the world had to give—beautiful, bright, healthy children, a reasonable amount of those qualities myself, a husband who loves and adores me and whom I adore in return, and all the things money could buy—he did this to prove to me it was worth nothing without him . . . and he succeeded.

I didn't know it, but this last detour was to be the most difficult of all—the bumpiest, dustiest, steepest and most confusing. But this detour was to be one of glory and victory. This detour had a rainbow at the end. This detour led me back to the main road for the last time . . . to Jesus Christ. Now that I have him, there are no more "detours" . . . but I will confess to you that my "road" is under frequent repair and construction!

Now that I am on the main road . . . now that I have a relationship with Jesus Christ . . . God is beginning to change me, to conform me to his image (though that will never be completed in this life). Materialism is one of the areas where the change is most noticeable to me. I never had huge appetites for things, but as I mature in Christ, my appetites and desires are changing, because I have truly learned that my happiness does not come from the treasures of this world but from the eternal security of Jesus Christ. Matthew said that our treasure is where our hearts are, and my treasure is in Jesus Christ.

I by no means intend to imply that God does not want us to enjoy what he has given us, but God never intended for us to place an overimportance on things. That goes for clothes, cars, food, work, intellect, people, football teams (for me it was my husband) . . . the list goes on forever. *He* wants to be the only God in our lives.

Another mask I wore was that of an extrovert—but an extrovert who had to try too hard. Everytime I went out, I spent hours beforehand pumping myself up for the big push. . . . This "push" meant struggling with deep anxieties about "what to wear, do I have the correct shoes and purse, what will I say, can I possibly be smart enough to fit into this crowd, can I possibly be chic enough to fit into that crowd, how can I make myself acceptable, how can I make myself lovable, can I fit in with anyone and everyone?" Inside I really was acceptable, but conveying this to others put me under tremendous pressure. Jesus Christ has changed all that. There are very few of the old fears and feelings of rejection, shyness, and inadequacy left in me. Today I am free to be who I am . . . and sometimes I am sad . . . often effervescent . . . occasionally pensive. Because Christ loves me, I have peace; because his love is the only important love. I am secure enough to accept that I don't always fit in, that *every*one isn't going to love me nor like me. Christ has made me free to be me. Whatever I feel, I am safe to feel it. (I am amazed more each day as the amount of myself I am able to share increases, not only the happy parts but those other parts—the sadness and despair of the past and the rough times of today! And that is exciting!)

The masks I wore were not suddenly yanked away. The Lord doesn't do things that way. He has slowly faded the masks away as what is underneath has been strengthened and matured by him enough to be revealed. Today what you see is what you get!

I could never have imagined the changes that have taken place in me until I experienced the unconditional love and acceptance of Christ. That love and acceptance freed me from my old feelings and fears. He is replacing fear and inadequacy with confidence. Anxiety is being replaced with a comfortableness about myself. The drive for approval from others is being tempered more each day with an easier acceptance of my faults and a more earnest appreciation for my virtues.

Another one of the ways he has changed me is that he has almost completely removed my virulent temper from my personality. I am truly amazed at the wonder of this miracle in my life. I was a screamer, a curser, and a bitter fighter . . . and how *much* I hurt myself with this travesty. I don't mean to overlook those I hurt . . . but for the most part, those other people love me . . . and I did not love me. The pain and guilt of those temper-tantrums only brought back in living color the old hopelessness of my past. I am grateful they are further and further apart and less and less a part of me.

But now for the most dramatic change God has made in me yet—the one the most evident to me but the least evident to others because I hid it so well. Abject despair no longer haunts me. I no longer wish to die or pray to die. I no longer *think* about dying. God has replaced that misery with a joy and a zeal for himself and for life that constantly amazes me! (Jeremiah 1:5 says, "I knew you before you were formed within your mother's womb. . . ." I believe that is so, and, therefore, God truly does have a purpose in my being on this earth. I'm here because he wants me here!)

I understand now that my temper and despair were symptoms of much deeper problems, and I am grateful to God for the counseling I have received—an important part of my growth—and for the love and support of Christian friends every day. I am grateful that the Lord has freed me enough to trust myself with a few safe people who will love and nurture me. Because my hurts ran so deeply, because I needed so much love, I have needed a number of friends who were able to love me that way . . . and God has provided those friends.

I am thankful, too, for my husband, who makes me want to stretch and grow and who stretches and grows with me. This is why I said earlier, this is where I had always longed to be. God gave me a husband who literally held on to me when I wanted to run . . . who holds and comforts me, something I had longed for all my life. Instead of running, I stay.

Our marriage is not always a rose garden. We've been through some tough times and will again, I am sure, because as I said earlier, we never get it all together in this life. Growth and change can be painful and unsettling, but there is a stability within us that cannot ever be shaken—a foundation that is ever beneath our feet, no matter how far we stray from it. This foundation is essential to our marriage relationship and is the reason we still have it!

I am particularly grateful for my two children. I am sure they were God's special gift to me, because without them and the Lord too I would have had no direction in my life. They were my anchor in the raging storm.

Both of my children are adults now, and each of them has a relationship with Jesus Christ. They have suffered a lot because of me and are deeply sensitive people, really beautiful young people with a maturing character and faith of their own. Life is a series of mountains and valleys, and I know that I must allow my children their valleys and trust God to use them to mature them just as he uses mine to mature me . . . to bring them to their own mountaintops with him.

There is something really special and exciting about sharing the struggles of life with my family now. As we develop and mature, we can really strengthen the bonds between us and our relationships become more meaningful than ever. It isn't horrible to have disappointments in the family relationships if the family can learn from the problems and create new ways (with the help of the Holy Spirit) to live within the new relationships.

Even though life can be painful at times, through Jesus Christ the pain is but a stepping stone. It is an exciting way to live . . . with this Lord of mine. Instead of facing defeat in every crisis, I can look forward to the victories that God gives out of those defeats. And I can learn to put my hand in his and know that he works all things together for good for those who love him (Rom. 8:28). It's a lot better than it was without him! Without him, life was impossible and hopeless. With him it is an adventure!

My parents divorced after over twenty years of marriage. My mother has undergone two cancer surgeries and my father has undergone one. Over a period of years, they both have accepted Christ, and because of him our relationships are more whole today than they have ever been. God *is* restoring the years the locusts have eaten in all areas of my life.

It's amazing to me that the testimony I gave just six months ago has already changed in so many ways. I am more aware of and open about sharing the hidden things about myself . . . and I thought I was pretty open six months ago! This amazing growth is a product of a lot of hard work.

One, I have worked very hard in my counseling . . . and I see how God has used it to deal with the buried garbage of my life. When all this is dredged up and looked at and dealt with, he is waiting with hands open to me to take it away forever. He never fails to pick up all I give him. He doesn't try to remove garbage I haven't put out for pick-up, but he does such a good job with what I give him that I am encouraged to keep it up. Well . . . what do you suppose he does with my garbage? (This is just too much!) He takes it and makes compost out of it! Compost is a natural fertilizer. Compost makes soil fertile, which makes plants bear more fruit.

Two, when I have not been in a Bible class, I have had my nose in the Bible a lot of the time. The Bible is the only real source for knowing God, and the more I know about him, the more I am able to believe about him and trust in him . . . and the more he reveals about himself to me.

Three, I have spent a great deal of time with God's family—the Body of Christ. This fellowship has been invaluable to me. It's the family I've always craved—the loving arms of a whole community.

By saying all this, I never mean to imply that Christians don't fail . . . because Christians are just people. We are subject to mistakes and lapses and even ignorances of our faith. Nor do I mean to imply that Christians shouldn't have secular friends, but my Christian friends have been a special source of strength to me because of their abundant love.

Perhaps your life hasn't been as tragic as mine and you don't identify with my particular story. Perhaps you have

gone through life with few problems and little suffering but
are wondering why you don't feel as good as you would
like. You're not sure what it is, but something just isn't quite
right. This is a whole different dilemma, because all who
aren't in a relationship with Jesus Christ experience a
vacuum within, and it is painful. And those who have no
labels for their pain are really stumped by it. So whether
you have labels or no labels, the vacuum exists in all of us,
and the answer is always the same. That answer is Jesus
Christ.

The roadblocks I set up to avoid accepting this answer
are just incredible! Perhaps you will recognize one or more
of them.

How many times I thought: "I'm just not ready to make
that kind of commitment. Just one or two more fun times
before I quit living it up, before I give up the 'good life,'
whatever that was! (For me it was the next husband.)
Maybe for you it's that bigger house, that super-sleek auto-
mobile, that maid three days a week. For a man, it might be
a promotion, a few more bucks in the bank, one more business deal! One of the most beautiful verses in the Bible,
Ephesians 3:20, promises that "God, by the action of his
power that is at work within us, is able to carry out his
purposes and do superabundantly far over and above all
that we dare ask or think . . . infinitely beyond our highest
prayers, desires, thoughts, hopes or dreams" (*Amplified
Bible*). The thrills of this world only left me hungry and
longing for more. They left me asking, "Is that all there is?"
The real glory has been in knowing and growing in Jesus
Christ. There is no earthly experience to compare to it . . .
no rapture so divine . . . no strength so intense . . . no
love so deep . . . no peace so sublime . . . no joy so grati-
fying.

How many times I thought: "I'm going to get my life
straightened out . . . then I'll get right with God!" Now
that *is* downright comical. I wonder . . . what was I waiting for? Remember in Jeremiah 29:11 where the Lord says,
"For I know the plans I have for you. They are plans for
good and not for evil, to give you a future and a hope."

How many times I thought: "I'm afraid to give control

of my life to God. What will happen? What will people
think? What if he made me do something I didn't want to
do! What if he made me teach a Bible class? What if people
thought I was a religious fanatic?" I know now that he
never *makes* us do anything. I never do anything that he
hasn't first given me the desire to do. Ezekiel 36:26 says, "And
I will give you a new heart—I will give you new and right
desires—and put a new spirit within you. I will take out
your stony hearts of sin and give you new hearts of love."
I *want* to tell people how great he is! I *want* to tell, not
because I am a religious fanatic but because he told us in
the Scriptures to tell about him. I *want* to tell because I love
him and he loves me and I want other people to know about
him. I feel like Paul, who said he was happy to be counted
a fool for Christ. He never changes a negative without
having a positive with which to replace it. And he *always*
changes me for the better (in his eyes), and only because
of him do I have the courage to change.

How many times I thought: "I'm not worthy . . . I'm not
good enough . . . I'm too sinful. . . ." And I was right. I'm
not worthy. I *am* too sinful. I can never be good enough.
But Jesus Christ does all those things for me. He makes
me worthy. He makes me good enough. He paid for my sins,
and when God looks at me, he sees Christ in me, not because
of anything I've done, but because of what he has done. 2
Corinthians 5:21 says, "For God took the sinless Christ and
poured into him our sins. Then, in exchange, he poured
God's goodness into us!"

He's so good! . . . And I praise him for my pain and
suffering and I praise him for my faults, because it all has
made me so sensitive to the need in my life for a Savior . . .
and so grateful for what he really did for me on that cross.

Well . . . what *did* he do for me? Romans 6:23 says that
he gave me a gift. All I had to do was receive it. This gift
was eternal life. It's not something I have to earn . . . nor
is it something I *can* earn. "The free gift of God is eternal
life in Christ Jesus."

(In a recent poll, statistics revealed that a large per-
centage of the world's population know about Jesus and
believe that he is the Son of God, yet they do not know how

to receive him . . . the gift . . . how to make him a real part of their lives . . . how to know him personally.)

How do you do that? Revelation 3:20 presents a beautiful picture of the way. "Look! I have been standing at the door [of your heart] and I am constantly knocking. If anyone hears me calling him and opens the door, I *will* come in and fellowship with him and he with me." John 14:23 says, "Jesus replied, 'Because I will only reveal myself to those who love me and obey me. The Father will love them too, and we will come to them and live with them.'"

These Scriptures are saying, "Invite me into your life. I will come live in you." That's how to make him real. John 14:6 says, "I am the way, the truth, and the life; no man cometh unto the Father, but by me."

Perhaps you've not given the Lord a lot of thought, or maybe you have and you are reaching for him but don't feel you have found him. . . . He still isn't real to you.

If you would like to pray the following prayer, you will not only gain eternal life with the Father, but you will begin the new adventure of living with Jesus Christ. You will never regret it!

Lord Jesus, I do not know you, but I want to know you. I confess to you that I am a sinner and I rejoice that you love me so much that even if I had been the only person on the entire earth, you would have died just for me. I invite you to come into my life . . . I choose you to be my Lord and Savior. I also ask you, Holy Spirit, to teach me what you want me to know and help me understand what you want me to understand. For it is in Jesus' precious name that I pray. Amen.

To the Nonbeliever

I GRIEVE so for those of you who reject Christ, but especially those who reject him on the basis of "intellectual" decisions or "gut" feelings without ever giving any serious study about the potential (for you) eternal life and death question of Jesus Christ. Yet, you give a lot of serious thought to the fact that you believe there is *no* God! Because you choose not to believe does not mean he does not exist or will go away!

C. S. Lewis, one of Christianity's most brilliant contemporary authors, was an outspoken atheist. Yet his conversion began with the question, What if he really does exist? We've all had this same thought many times, and it is placed within us by the Holy Spirit. Sheldon Vanauken, a young friend of C. S. Lewis at Oxford University, was also an atheist (briefly) and a confirmed agnostic for quite some time. His conversion began with the subtle realization that his belief in no God was as much a religion for him as believing *in* God. Again, the Holy Spirit was "nudging" him to pursue God in all his fullness.

Christ beckons to us daily, yet so many of us refuse to listen to his gentle nudges . . . but that's how it begins! Don't you think that it's worth considering that there very well may be a God and that there also may be an after-life? And don't you think it's well worth giving a lot of thought to the fact that we might have a choice about where we spend that after-life? Because we do!

Jesus Christ, the God-Man, made some pretty astonishing statements about himself in the four Gospels. He would have to have been crazy to have made those statements if they weren't true, and yet he behaved like anything *but* a crazy

man. Instead, he backed up his pronouncements with action!
In John 10:30 he said, "I and my Father are one." John
14:8–9 says, "Philip said, 'Sir, show us the Father and we will
be satisfied.' Jesus replied, 'Don't you even know who I am,
Philip, even after all this time I have been with you? Anyone who has seen me has seen the Father! So why are you
asking to see him?' " Jesus said he forgives our sins . . . and
I think it would help to look at the translation of the Greek
word for *forgive, Aphiemi:* "the remission of the punishment
due to sinful conduct, the deliverance of the sinner from the
penalty divinely, and therefore righteously, imposed; such
remission is based upon the vicarious and propitiatory sacrifice of Christ."

Mark 2:1–12, "Several days later he returned to Capernaum,
    and the news of his arrival spread quickly through the
    city. Soon the house where he was staying was so packed
    with visitors that there wasn't room for a single person
    more, not even outside the door. And he preached the
    Word to them. Four men arrived carrying a paralyzed
    man on a stretcher. They couldn't get to Jesus through the
    crowd, so they dug through the clay roof above his head
    and lowered the sick man on his stretcher, right down in
    front of Jesus. When Jesus saw how strongly they believed
    that he would help, Jesus said to the sick man, 'Son, your
    sins are forgiven!' But some of the Jewish religious leaders
    said to themselves as they sat there, 'What? This is blas-
    phemy! *Does he think he is God? For only God can forgive
    sins.'* Jesus could read their minds and said to them at
    once, 'Why does this bother you? *I, the Messiah, have the
    authority on earth to forgive sins.* But talk is cheap—
    anybody could say that. So I'll prove it to you by healing
    this man.' Then, turning to the paralyzed man, he com-
    manded, 'Pick up your stretcher and go on home, for you
    are healed!' The man jumped up, took the stretcher, and
    pushed his way through the stunned onlookers! Then how
    they praised God. 'We've never seen anything like this
    before!' they all exclaimed."

Jesus had credibility! Everywhere people flocked to Him!
. . . But the most remarkable statement Jesus made was
that he was the Way.

John 14:6, "I am the Way—yes, and the Truth and the Life. *No one can get to the Father except by means of me.*" I *know* he's there! He has revealed too much of himself to me. To question is out of the question for me. But, then, I've also done a lot of studying and praying and talking with other believers, and today I would gladly give up all that I have for him, and in worldly terms, I have a lot to give up.

My relationship with him is the only thing that has any real value to me, because without him, I am back in the same old mess I was before, and I never ever want to be there again! Because of my relationship with him, I am a better wife, mother, and friend. He has taken nothing good from these relationships, but he has added abundantly to each one, including, and especially, my relationship with myself.

Another one of the sadnesses for me is for those of you, and I include myself in this category, who have been turned off of Jesus Christ because of "religion." For years I sat in churches of all denominations searching . . . but wondering what in the world I was doing there. What was I seeking? Why couldn't I ever find it? Many people go to church because it's the "thing to do." Today, I know that Jesus Christ *is* the church. Now I can sit in any Christian church and know why I am there. Jesus Christ is not a religion. Jesus Christ is a man, but a man who is God. I am not "religious." I am a Christian, and therein lies the difference.

God has placed within each of us a void which can only be filled by him. The problem is, we get sidetracked along the way. We try to fill that void with so many other things— human relationships, religions, philosophy, wealth, power, knowledge, chemicals (drugs and alcohol), sex, to name just a few. Yet none of these truly fills the void; rather, it increases the void . . . makes it bigger and emptier . . . thereby making one more insecure.

As I look back in my own life, and as I observe the lives of others, through personal relationships as well as in the media, I see so much empty seeking going on. So many people looking so many places! I tried to fill that void with a multitude of things. In fact, I didn't miss much along the way, but the only thing that ever gave me peace, the only

thing that ended the search—and changed my life—was
Jesus Christ.

At this point, all I'm asking you to do is open yourself up
to the gentle nudges of the Holy Spirit. Give him a sincere
chance to reveal himself to you.

Jeremiah 29:13 promises, "You will find me when you seek
me, *if you look for me in earnest."*

*O Lord, I know that you genuinely delight in revealing
yourself to those who sincerely seek to know you. Father, I
just pray that as your children read this book their hearts
will be sensitive to the nudges of the Holy Spirit . . . that
they will know they have been touched by you. In your
precious Son's name, we pray. Amen.*

MILK FOR BABES:
A Biblical Foundation for New Christians

1 Peter 2:2: "As newborn babes, desire the sincere *milk of the Word,* that ye may grow thereby."

Matthew 11:28–30: "Come unto me, all ye that labor and are heavy laden, and I will give you rest. Take my yoke upon you, and *learn of me.* . . ."

Jeremiah 15:16: "Thy words [spiritual food] were found, and I did eat them, and thy word was unto me the joy and rejoicing of mine heart. . . ."

THE TITLE AND subject matter of this study book arose out of my own need for follow-up material for new Christians who have no classes readily available to them, and who, perhaps, have no other Christian friends with whom they can share and study.

I have a precious friend in the San Francisco Bay area who accepted Christ and was so eager to share her new-found faith with her friends. One night she called me, excited but distressed. "Anne, help! All my friends want to know about Jesus, and I've shared my experience with them, but I don't know where to go from there! I don't know what else to tell them." She had no other Christian friends and didn't even know a good church to attend, so I began writing Bible-teaching letters to her in San Francisco and to her daughter in France who had also accepted Christ. When this letter-writing ministry grew too large for me, my next thought was to write a series of lessons and make photocopies of them to send to my many friends, but that seemed so very impersonal. Thus, the seed for this book began to grow, and with it a strong desire to put into *simple* form answers to questions that many people have.

I looked and looked for a book which might even come
close, but my frustration continued. In the meantime, at
home, my husband was asking questions on almost a daily
basis. In fact, he should share credit for this book with me
because he says I could never have written it had he not
"asked all those questions." It has been a joyful sharing
experience with him, for which I am deeply grateful. My
prayer for each of you reading this book is that God will
send new friends in Christ to you with whom you can have
fellowship. In the meantime, count me as one of the first in
the ever-broadening circle.

The information available here is basic to the strength of
every Christian, and if you will study slowly and carefully,
you will receive a firm foundation upon which to build. It is
only through knowing God's Word that we can grow in our
relationship with him. The quality and growth of that relationship are directly related to the quantity and quality of
our Bible study, because the Bible is the way God has
chosen to communicate with man.

Through studying God's Word, you will discover that he
never changes. The God on the first page of Genesis is the
same God as the one on the last page of Revelation. He re-
mains constant and consistent. You will also learn that the
men of the Old Testament were saved exactly the same way
the men of the New Testament are saved—by faith.

Milk for Babes is not a book to be read in an afternoon, for
that would not accomplish in you what you need or want.
Look at it this way: You wouldn't pour a quart of milk down
a new baby's throat, would you? In the same way, this carefully prepared formula for new babes in Christ should be
taken in small but meaningful portions each day. In order to
grow, babies must be fed a well-balanced diet every day.
Christian babes too must be fed on a regular basis; in fact,
Christians of *any* age need a regular diet of spiritual food.
Why? Because you are not just studying the Bible; you are
getting to know God in a deep, personal and intimate way.
Knowing *anyone* deeply, personally, and intimately takes a
lot of quality time.

(By the way, if it annoys you a little bit to be called a
"babe" in Christ, let me reassure you that I am only two and

a half years old in the Lord at this writing and am still very much a babe in many areas.)

Remember, too, that no two Christians agree on every single point. There are basic truths, but within those truths there are shades and nuances. All anyone can do is share as much truth as he or she has.

As a Christian, I am changing subtly in my understanding daily. And if I am changing daily, then certainly I can never expect others to agree with me totally, because they, too, are changing daily. The Christian experience is an ongoing one, and one in which we hope we will be growing and changing and learning until we die.

I feel very secure about my beliefs. I feel so secure that I don't have to make you believe exactly what I believe in order to feel good about myself or about you. Therefore, I ask that you accept this book as it has been written . . . out of my love and desire to share my joy in Christ. Take what you want and leave the rest . . . perhaps for another day.

What I am really trying to say is that you may come to some things which are difficult for you to believe or understand. Don't give up on the Lord because of human differences. Just "hang them on a hook" and ask the Holy Spirit to teach you what he wants you to know and help you understand what he wants you to understand. That way you can't go wrong. He has a way of opening it all up to us a little at a time.

Unless otherwise noted, all of the Scriptures used in this book are from *The Living Bible,* which is a paraphrase of a translation. A translation is a word-for-word exchange from one language to another. A paraphrase is an interpretation, or, more specifically, a translation that has been put into one's own words. The reason I have chosen *The Living Bible* is that it is the clearest and easiest for most new Christians to understand. (When I use the King James Version instead, I will notate it "KJV.")

Please note that in this book, all use of italics within Scripture passages is for emphasis and is mine. All comments in brackets are for clarity and are mine, unless otherwise noted.

As you study, why don't you get out your Bible and underline and meditate on each verse given. (I underline with a felt-tipped pen and make notes with a ball-point pen. My Bible is underlined and scribbled all over—a part of me.) This will also help you familiarize yourself with the Bible. Most Bibles have indexes in front to help you locate the various books. Many of you reading this book may have come from backgrounds that gave you no firsthand acquaintance with the Bible, and since there are so many things to show about the relationship between Old and New Testament Scriptures, I've identified all the Old Testament verses with an OT next to them in the margin. The other verses are New Testament, of course. I hope those of you who already know the Bible will bear with us and not let that be a distraction, knowing how much this will help many of our new Christian brothers and sisters in their study.

One of the things that Satan has used to keep people away from the Bible is the idea that it is dull and dry! In truth, God is very serious about every word, but it is not dull and dry! I am sure that no one has a greater sense of humor than God, and the Bible is full to overflowing with it. It's a way of seeing I did not have until I became his.

I ask you to remember that God made us in his image: "And God said, let us make man in our image, after our likeness . . ." (Gen. 1:26, KJV). God has given me a sense of humor and I was created in his image. I believe in having fun with him and feel very comfortable about that!

I also believe in reverence for God. I feel about him exactly the way John did on the Island of Patmos when Christ appeared to him. "And when I saw him, *I fell at his feet as dead . . .*" (Rev. 1:7). John was so awed by the majesty and beauty of our righteous Lord that he could only fall in a heap at his feet. When I think and meditate on that same majesty and beauty, I often fall to my knees in wonder, love and gratitude.

A dear friend, Sandra Hulse, a beautiful Christian lady, wrote the following poem as a result of a conversation she and I had, and so she shared it with me:

> Spirit's transparent thread, weaves through death's
>   pale and bitter door.
> Breath caught—crushed to nothingness—a non-
>   existent void.

Soul—
 a
  broken
   stone.
In Resurrection's blinding brilliance—The Light!
 Transforms.
I heap the Abundant Treasure of my life—His
 gift to me—
At His pierced and precious feet.
Press His spotless garment to my mouth.
His Priceless Blood I bear.
My Lover!—My Lord!
My Song!—
My Heart's Delight!—
 Caught up in Flight to Bliss!!

I weep for joy at the awesomeness of my Lord, Jesus Christ! I weep for joy for the love and generosity of my friend, Sandra Hulse, and many others, for making me feel a part of that beautiful expression of love and reverence. His goodness abounds!

Oh! There is so much for which to be thankful!

Heavenly Father, I praise you for the one who is reading this book. I pray, dear Lord, that you will reveal through your Holy Spirit all that you want this child of yours to know about you. Give this little one understanding and wisdom and a hunger to know you through your Word. And, Father, please provide guidance and encouragement through these pages, and instill a patience and quietness of spirit within him or her that the truth and beauty of your word may be planted in his or her soul forever. In Jesus' Name. Amen.

A Few Definitions Might Help

LIFE = *Spiritual life; eternal life with God.* Life begins the moment you accept Christ as Lord and Savior.

John 10:28: "*And I give unto them eternal life; and they shall never perish,* neither shall any man pluck them out of my hand" (KJV).

Romans 8:11: "And if the Spirit of God, who raised up Jesus from the dead, lives in you, *he will make your dying bodies live again after you die,* by means of this same Holy Spirit living within you."

DEATH = *Spiritual death.* Spiritual death pertains to those who have never accepted Jesus Christ as Lord and Savior. If this "state" continues until physical death, the soul passes into hell. A spiritually dead person is a sinner who has not accepted the payment for his sins by the death of Jesus Christ. This is Satan's realm and that is why the unsaved are frequently referred to in Scripture as "evil men."

OT *Habakkuk 2:4:* "Note this: *Wicked men [nonbelievers] trust themselves alone, and fail [die];* but the righteous man [believer] trusts in me and lives!"

John 10:10: "*The thief's [the devil's] purpose is to steal [from God], kill and destroy.* My [Christ's] purpose is to give life in all its fullness."

HEAVEN = *Where God, the Father, Son and Holy Spirit are;* where we who have accepted Christ as Lord and Savior will be when we physically die.

Mark 11:25: ". . . so that your *Father in heaven* will forgive you your sins too."

John 3:13: "For only I, *the Messiah,* have come to earth and will return to heaven again."

1 Peter 1:12: ". . . through the *Holy Spirit sent from heaven,* things into which angels long to look . . ." (RSV). Heaven is described in Revelation 7:16–17: *"They will never be hungry again, nor thirsty, and they will be fully protected from the scorching noontime heat.* For the Lamb [Jesus] standing in front of the throne will feed them and be their Shepherd and lead them to the springs of the Water of Life. And God will wipe their tears away."

HELL = Need I say more?

Luke 16:23–31: ". . . his soul went into hell. There, in torment, he saw Lazarus in the far distance with Abraham. 'Father Abraham,' he shouted, 'have some pity! Send Lazarus over here if only to dip the tip of his finger in water and cool my tongue, for I am in anguish in these flames.' But Abraham said to him, 'Son, remember that during your lifetime you had everything you wanted [you did it your way], and Lazarus had nothing. So now he is here being comforted and you are in anguish. And besides, there is a great chasm separating us, and anyone wanting to come to you from here [heaven] is stopped at its edge; and no one over there can cross to us.' Then the rich man said, 'O Father Abraham, then please send him to my father's home—for I have five brothers—to warn them about this place of torment lest they come here when they die.' But Abraham said, 'The Scriptures have warned them again and again. Your brothers can read them any time they want to.' The rich man replied, 'No, Father Abraham, they won't bother to read them. But if someone is sent to them from the dead, then they will turn from their sins.' But Abraham said, 'If they won't listen to Moses and the prophets [in the Scriptures], they won't listen even though someone rises from the dead.' " [Jesus rose from the dead, and still most people don't listen.]

2 Thessalonians 1:9: ". . . the penalty of eternal destruction, *away from the presence of the Lord"* (RSV).

KINGDOM OF GOD = *The rule of God in the hearts of men;* the result of a personal relationship with Jesus Christ; begins the moment you invite him into your life and continues throughout eternity.

Luke 17:21: "You won't be able to say, 'It has begun here in this place or there in that part of the country.' For *the Kingdom of God is within you.*"

Mark 4:11: "He replied, 'You are permitted to know some truths about the Kingdom of God that are hidden to those outside the Kingdom.'"

RIGHTEOUSNESS = *Perfection; the state of being perfectly perfect.* God himself is the only one who has this attribute of perfection. He would not be God without it.

OT   *Isaiah 45:19:* "I publicly proclaim bold promises; I do not whisper obscurities in some dark corner so that no one can know what I mean. And I didn't tell Israel to ask me for what I didn't plan to give! No, for *I, Jehovah, speak only truth and righteousness.*"

OT   *Psalm 71:19:* "Thy righteousness also, O God, is very high, who has done great things: O God, who is like unto thee!" (KJV). [No one is like you, God!]

1 John 2:1: "My little children, I am telling you this so that you will stay away from sin. But if you sin, there is someone to plead for you before the Father. His name is *Jesus Christ, the one who is all that is good and who pleases God completely.*" [Without Jesus Christ, we are sinners in the eyes of God.]

Romans 3:10: "As it is written, *There is none righteous, no not one*" (KJV).

We will find out later, though, in this book under the section, "Christ Made Me Worthy," just how God rectifies the mess of the life of a sinner by *giving to us* the righteousness of Christ.

FEAR OF GOD = *Reverential awe; not terror; an attitude of deep respect; this includes a deep sense of accountability before God; a profound awareness of "who we are" as opposed to "who he is."*

OT   *Proverbs 9:10:* "For the reverence and fear of God are basic to all wisdom. Knowing God results in every other kind of understanding."

OT **Proverbs 1:7:** "The fear of the Lord is the beginning of knowledge . . ." (KJV).

OT **Proverbs 14:26–27:** "In the fear of the Lord is strong confidence: and his children shall have a place of refuge. The fear of the Lord is a fountain of life, to depart from the snares of death" (KJV).

1 John 4:18: "We need have no fear of someone who loves us perfectly [as only God does]; his perfect love for us eliminates all dread of what He might do to us. If we are afraid, it is for fear of what he might do to us, and shows that we are not fully convinced that he really loves us."

ISRAEL = *Symbolic of the individual believer today.* For our purposes, in order to understand Scripture, it is essential to know this. In most cases, when the word *Israel* appears, you may substitute your own name in its place. At times, of course, *Israel* refers specifically to the nation.

Galatians 3:6–9: "Abraham had the same experience—God declared him fit for heaven only because he believed God's promises. You can see from this that *the real children of Abraham are all the men of faith who truly trust in God.* What's more, the Scriptures looked forward to this time when God would save the Gentiles also, through their faith. God told Abraham about this long ago when he said, *'I will bless those in every nation who trust in me as you do.' And so it is: all who trust in Christ share the same blessing Abraham received.'*

(In the chapter entitled "Why are the Jews God's Chosen Ones?" we will trace Jesus Christ's genealogy back to Abraham through his "seed," Isaac. Thus, God blessed every nation through Abraham. See Luke 3:23–38.)

Romans 2:28–29: "For you are not real Jews just because you were born of Jewish parents or because you have gone through the Jewish initiation ceremony of circumcision. No, *a real Jew is anyone whose heart is right with God.* . . ."

Romans 11:17: "But some of these branches from Abraham's tree, some of the Jews, have been broken off. And you Gentiles who were branches from, we might say, a wild olive tree, were grafted in. So now you, too, receive the

blessing God has promised Abraham and his children,
sharing in God's rich nourishment of his own special olive
tree."

*Sweet heavenly Father, as we come to the chapter on
your Word, I pray you will especially open the heart of the
one studying to the importance of your Word and the
beauty and truth on every page. I pray also that you will use
these pages to reveal yourself, my Lord. In Christ's name I
pray. Amen.*

The Word of God: Our Only Authority

BEFORE I RECEIVED Jesus Christ, I had personally given the Bible *very* bad reviews. It seemed contradictory, unsavory, unpalatable and thus quite dull. There was *no* book I was *less* interested in than the Bible. I had very strong opinions about its authenticity and validity. To my human mind the Bible was basically bunk. It contained some rather nice words of wisdom, some sound philosophy, but words actually from God? Bunk! Since accepting Jesus Christ and receiving his Holy Spirit, the Bible has begun to unfold to me in a magnificent way. I now see it as the love letter God intends it to be to his children.

How did Jesus Christ and his indwelling Holy Spirit make a difference? Well, as usual, God says it so much better than I . . .

1 Corinthians 1:18–2:16: "I know very well how foolish it sounds to those who are lost, when they hear that Jesus died to save them. But we who are saved recognize this message as the very power of God. For God says, 'I will destroy all human plans of salvation no matter how wise they seem to be, and ignore the best ideas of men, even the most brilliant of them.'

"So what about these wise men, these scholars, these brilliant debaters of this world's great affairs? God has made them all look foolish, and shown their wisdom to be useless nonsense. For God in his wisdom saw to it that the world would never find God through human brilliance, and then he stepped in and saved all those who believed his message, which the world calls foolish and silly. It seems foolish to the Jews because they want a sign from heaven as proof that what is preached is true; and it is foolish to the Gentiles because they believe only what agrees with their philosophy and seems wise to them. So when we preach about Christ dying to save them, the Jews are offended and the Gentiles say it's all nonsense. But God has opened the eyes of those called to salvation, both Jews and Gentiles, to see that Christ is the mighty power of God to save them; Christ himself is the center of God's wise plan for their salvation. This so-called 'foolish' plan of God is far wiser than the wisest plan of the wisest man, and God in his weakness—Christ dying on the cross—is far stronger than any man.

"Notice among yourselves, dear brothers, that few of you who follow Christ have big names or power or wealth. Instead, God has deliberately chosen to use ideas the world considers foolish and of little worth in order to shame those people considered by the world as wise and great. He has chosen a plan despised by the world, counted as nothing at all, and used it to bring down to nothing those the world considers great, *so that no one anywhere can ever brag in the presence of God.*

"*For it is from God alone that you have your life through Christ Jesus.* He showed us God's plan of salvation; *he was the one who made us acceptable to God; he made us pure and holy and gave himself to purchase our salvation. As it says in the Scriptures, 'If anyone is going to boast, let him boast only of what the Lord has done.'*

"Dear brothers, even when I first came to you I didn't use lofty words and brilliant ideas to tell you God's message. For I decided that I would speak only of Jesus Christ and his death on the cross. I came to you in weakness—timid and trembling. And my preaching was very plain, not with a lot of oratory and human wisdom, but the Holy Spirit's power was in my words, proving to those who heard them that the message was from God. I did this because I wanted your faith to stand firmly upon God, not on man's great ideas.

"Yet when I am among mature Christians I do speak with words of great wisdom, but not the kind that comes from here on earth and not the kind that appeals to the great men of this world, who are doomed to fall. Our words are wise because they are from God, telling of God's wise plan to bring us into the glories of heaven. This plan was hidden in former times [in the Old Testament], though it was made for our benefit before the world began. But the great men of the world have not understood it; if they had, they would never have crucified the Lord of Glory.

"That is what is meant by the Scriptures which say that no mere man has ever seen, heard or even imagined what wonderful things God has ready for those who love the Lord. But we know about these things because God has sent his Spirit to tell us, and his Spirit searches out and shows us all of God's deepest secrets. No one can really know what anyone else is thinking, or what he is really like, except that person himself. And no one can know God's thoughts except God's own Spirit. And God has actually given us his Spirit (not the world's spirit) to tell us about the wonderful free gifts of grace and blessing that God has given us. In telling you about these gifts we have even used the very words given to us by the Holy Spirit, not words that we as men might choose. So we use the Holy Spirit's words to explain the Holy Spirit's facts. But the man who isn't a Christian can't understand and can't accept these thoughts from God, which the Holy Spirit teaches us. They sound foolish to him, because only those who have the Holy Spirit within them can understand what the Holy Spirit means. Others just can't take it in.

"But the spiritual man has insight into everything, and that bothers and baffles the man of the world, who can't understand him at all. How could he? For certainly he has never been one to know the Lord's thoughts, or to discuss them with him, or to move the hands of God by prayer. *But strange as it seems, we Christians actually do have within us a portion of the very thoughts and mind of Christ."*

These verses speak more powerfully to me now than they ever have and are some of the mightiest in the Bible. In fact, it really awes me that my mind has been "wired in" to God's mind through his Holy Spirit, and I *know* that's true because of what has happened to my life. The Bible speaks to me as truth now. I could meditate on 1 Corinthians 2:10–12 and the last sentence in 1 Corinthians 2:16 every day and never lose the thrill of its impact. Believers are given the mind of Jesus Christ, the mind of God himself, and he makes his wisdom available to us. There is no way to explain it to you beyond this. The best way to understand it is to experience it.

It's a difficult thing to do—to put aside one's own pride of intellect where God is concerned—but I invite you to consider just that. After all, what can you lose if it's just between you and your God? For Jesus said that we *must* come as little children and that is so difficult to do.

Matthew 18:3–4: "And [Jesus] said, 'Unless you turn to God from your sins and become as little children, you will never get into the Kingdom of Heaven. Therefore *anyone who humbles himself as this little child, is the greatest in the Kingdom of Heaven.'* "

Let's look at it from another perspective. Let's look at it from Jesus' perspective. When Jesus was conceived by the Holy Spirit in Mary's womb, he literally "emptied" himself of his position as equal to God the Father and Holy Spirit. This "emptying" was in *no* way an emptying of his divinity, but rather *was* the taking on of humanity. By doing this, he put himself in the position of being *dependent upon* God rather than *equal to* God.

Philippians 2:5–8: "Let this mind be in you, which was also in Christ Jesus: who being in the form of God, thought it not robbery to be equal with God: but made of himself no reputation, and took upon him the form of a servant, and was made in the likeness of men: and being found in fashion as a man, he humbled himself, and became obedient unto death, even the death of the cross" (KJV).

God does not require us to "empty" ourselves of our intellects, for most intellectuals really know about God in *some* way . . . they have some awareness of him. It is the *pride of intellect* which often gets in the way of understanding him more fully and it is the *pride of intellect* which we must empty ourselves of. Pride of intellect tells us that we can know everything about God! And that simply is not possible.

Just as Jesus so glorified his Father by emptying himself, so can we glorify and honor God the Father, Son, and Holy Spirit, by emptying ourselves of our pride of intellect and opening ourselves up to the tremendous truths of God, the greatest of which was Jesus Christ.

John 14:6: "Jesus told him, 'I am the Way—yes, and *the Truth* and the Life. . . .'"

By opening ourselves up to the truths of God, he then can enable us to reach the potential he has given us, to be as he intends us to be. 1 Corinthians 1:18—2:16 speaks so beautifully to that!

I invite you to come as a little child to the throne of God.

Hebrews 4:16: "So let us come boldly to the very throne of God and stay there to receive his mercy and to find grace to help us in our times of need."

Earlier I said that God's Word is the way he has chosen to reveal himself to man. It is also the only thing we can truly count on. The Scriptures under this section confirm that this is true.

After I received Jesus Christ and began to really search the Word of God in a sincere and prayerful way, it initially seemed like a million riddles, none of which related to another. As I have pursued God's Truth with the guidance of the Holy Spirit, I see how wrong I was and how perfect God's Word really is! It's perfectly perfect! I have, in my finite way, attempted to illustrate just *how* perfect with the following example:

Visualize a jigsaw puzzle. Now visualize one hundred jigsaw puzzles stacked one on top of another. Every piece fits perfectly together in each of those puzzles to create an image. Now stretch your imagination and picture those puzzles not only linked together horizontally, but vertically! Each piece is separate, yet connected perfectly with the surrounding pieces—vertically *and* horizontally! Yet, if you take a piece out here and a piece out there, it does not present a clear picture. *Now* stretch your mind even further and view that puzzle from God's perspective. He is not limited by the human, finite mind; he knows no limits of time and space. Expand that puzzle horizontally and vertically in every direction into infinity. That's how perfect he is and how perfect his Word is. I don't ask you to believe it just yet. It merely illustrates my point. One can make the Bible look foolish by pulling words and verses out of context. But the Bible is integrally linked and meshed together and its teachings cannot be taken out of context.

I'd like to encourage skeptics and cynics of all kinds to "hang in there, baby" through the entire book and see the truth of these statements. Catch a glimpse of the wonders and mysteries of God which are here for you (especially in the second section of the book—"From Milk to Junior Food to Solid Food") if you are seeking in even the smallest way.

I would like to say here that this does not mean that I understand everything in the Bible. If I could understand everything in the Bible, then I could understand everything about God, and you and I both know that that is not possible. There *are* things in the Bible that no one understands, but that does not mean that they are not true! If I could understand everything about God, then he would not be divine. If I could, therefore, understand everything in the Bible, it would not be divinely inspired.

Kenneth Boa said in his book *God, I Don't Understand,* "It would be the height of egotism for a person to say that because an idea in the Bible does not make sense [does not conform to his reasoning], it cannot be true and the Bible must be in error on this point. Yet, men try to judge the Bible instead of letting it judge them. They try to approach God on their own terms, wanting to tell him how to operate and who to be." *

Over and over in the Bible God tells us it is his Word, and that, though it is written by men, they were writing what he wanted them to write, in order that he might reveal himself to his people.

2 Timothy 3:16: "The whole Bible was given to us by inspiration from God and is useful to teach us what is true and to make us realize what is wrong in our lives; it straightens us out and helps us do what is right."

Hebrews 1:1: "Long ago God spoke in many different ways

* Wheaton, Ill.: Victor Books, 1976, p. 14

to our fathers through the prophets [in visions, dreams, and even face to face], telling them little by little about his plans" (brackets not mine).

1 Thessalonians 2:13: "And we will never stop thanking God for this: that when we preached to you, you didn't think of the words we spoke as being just our own, but you accepted what we said as the very Word of God— which, of course, it was—and it changed your lives when you believed it."

2 Peter 1:20–21: "For no prophecy recorded in Scripture was ever thought up by the prophet himself. It was the Holy Spirit within these godly men who gave them true messages from God."

God's Word is spiritual food he has given us to feed our souls and mature us.

Romans 15:4: "These things that were written in the Scriptures so long ago are to teach us patience and to encourage us. . . ."

Romans 10:17: "So then faith cometh by hearing, and hearing by the Word of God" (KJV).

Matthew 4:4: "But Jesus told him, 'No! For the Scriptures tell us that bread won't feed men's souls: obedience to every word of God is what we need.'"

OT *Jeremiah 15:16:* "Thy words were found, and I did eat them, and thy Word was unto me the joy and rejoicing of mine heart . . ." (KJV).

John 17:17: "Make them pure and holy through teaching them your words of truth."

OT *Isaiah 45:23: "I have sworn by myself and I will never go back on my word, for it is true—that every knee in all the world shall bow to me, and every tongue shall swear allegiance to my name."*

OT *Psalm 119:105:* "Thy Word is a lamp unto my feet, and a light unto my path" (KJV).

John 15:3: "Now ye are clean through the Word which I have spoken to you" (KJV).

OT *Psalm 119:11:* "I have thought much about your words, and stored them in my heart so that they would hold me back from sin."

God's Word is as relevant today as it was when it was given. The Bible is a very contemporary book—timeless.

Matthew 24:35: "Heaven and earth [the universe] will disappear, but my words remain forever."

OT   *Psalm 119:160:* "Thy Word is true from the beginning, and every one of thy righteous ordinances endureth forever" (KJV).

OT   *Psalm 119:89:* "Forever, O Lord, your Word stands firm in heaven."

OT   *Isaiah 40:8:* "The grass withers, the flowers fade, but the Word of our God shall stand forever."

And now for something very profound for you to consider. Jesus Christ is the Word.

John 1:1–2: "In the beginning was the Word, and the Word was with God, and the Word was God. The same was in the beginning with God" (KJV).

John 1:14: "And the Word was made flesh and dwelt among us, (and we beheld His glory, the glory as of the only begotten of the Father,) full of grace and truth" (KJV).

Jesus Christ is on every page of the Old and New Testaments. I don't expect you to believe that at this early stage, but the more you study the Bible, the clearer this will become. Later, in the chapters entitled "Prophecy in the Old Testament" and "Types and Shadows of Christ in the Old Testament" we will take a look at just a small portion of Christ in the Old Testament.

Before we move on to the next chapter, I'd like to share with you that the Bible study which went into the writing of this book has spiritually fed me and greatly enlarged my view of God and richly blessed my life. It has taught me. I hope you also may be enriched by reading it.

God's Word is the only authority we have for knowing him and what he wants for us and from us. Never take my word or the word of anyone else as truth. Make us prove it to you with the Word of God! Even then, ask the Holy Spirit to reveal to **you** *his* truth.

When studying the Bible, never take Scripture out of context. It is essential to read the entire section surrounding a verse and to ask the questions, "To whom is this section being addressed?" "Is this being said to believers or non-believers?" "Who is speaking?"

One last reminder—and this cannot be said too often—it isn't advisable to study the Bible without first going to the Lord in prayer for the guidance and revelation of the Holy Spirit.

Colossians 1:9: "For this cause we also, since the day we heard it [of your conversion], do not cease to pray for you, and to *desire that ye might be filled with the knowledge of his will in all wisdom and spiritual understanding*" (KJV).

That's what *Milk for Babes* is all about—the wonder and adventure of knowing the Lord through His Word.

OT *Isaiah 34:16:* "Seek ye out of the book of the Lord, and read . . ." (KJV).

Dear Lord, I thank you for your beautiful Word . . . and I especially thank you for Jesus Christ, the Living Word. Father, I beseech you to give your babes a hunger for you and your Word. Give them a love for your Word that grows with every passing day. Make the Word live to them. And, dear Lord, for those who are still seeking, I pray you will give them eyes to see and ears to hear. Speak to their hearts as only you can. In Jesus' name I pray. Amen.

God Is Not a Policeman in the Sky Keeping Score Against You; God Is Just, Loving and Merciful

I SUPPOSE I WAS at one time one of those millions of folks who view God as someone "up there somewhere" keeping a great big list of all my sins. "Oops! Annie did it again! Uh-oh! There goes another one onto Annie's list!" No wonder we don't want any part of God if we have this perspective of him! This scared me to death!

Scripture has revealed to me who God really is . . . and He is not The Great Scorekeeper in the Sky. He knows me and cherishes me. He desires greatly to make my life beautiful and good and rich.

Later in this book in the chapter entitled "The Results of Sin—Why We Need a Savior," we will take a quick look at the wrathful side of God, but, for now, trust me when I say that that side of God is directed strictly toward those who refuse to believe and truly accept his precious Son Jesus Christ—to those who deny him.

If you are wondering about all those people in the Old Testament who did not yet have Jesus Christ's death to pay for their sins, you will discover that, though it is true that they did not yet have him, they were saved by faith and by the promise of the Messiah to come. So they had the same redemption then that we have today. Theirs was in the Messiah to come and ours is in the Messiah Jesus Christ who came and died for us almost two thousand years ago.

Okay! Okay! I can almost hear you asking: But what about those people who *never* hear about Jesus Christ? What happens to them? I don't have a pat answer to this question, but in the next chapter I'll tell you what I think.

For now, let's take a look at the God who is just, loving and merciful!

OT *Psalm 34:8–9:* "Put God to the test and see how kind he is! See for yourself the way his mercies shower down on all who trust in him. If you belong to the Lord, reverence him; for everyone who does this has everything he needs."

OT *Psalm 121:3–4:* "He will never let me stumble, slip or fall. For he is always watching, never sleeping."

OT *Psalm 139:17–18:* "How precious it is, Lord, to realize that you are thinking about me constantly! I can't even count how many times a day your thoughts turn towards me. And when I waken in the morning, you are still thinking of me!"

OT *Deuteronomy 33:27:* "The eternal God is your Refuge, /And underneath are the everlasting arms. . . ."

OT *Deuteronomy 32:11:* "He spreads his wings over them,/ Even as an eagle overspreads her young./She carries them upon her winds—/As does the Lord his people!"

OT *Psalm 119:64:* "O Lord, the earth is full of your lovingkindness! . . ."

OT *Psalm 63:3:* "For your love and kindness are better to me than life itself. . . ."

OT *Isaiah 54:8:* "In a moment of anger I turned my face a little while; but with everlasting love I will have pity on you, says the Lord, your Redeemer."

OT *Jeremiah 31:3:* "For long ago the Lord had said to Israel: I have loved you, O my people, with an everlasting love; with lovingkindness I have drawn you to me."

OT *Psalm 66:20:* "Blessed be God who didn't turn away when I was praying, and didn't refuse me his kindness and love."

OT *Psalm 92:12–15:* "But the godly [believers] shall flourish like palm trees, and grow tall as the cedars of Lebanon. For they are transplanted into the Lord's own garden, and are under his personal care. Even in old age they will still produce fruit and be vital and green. This honors the Lord, and exhibits his faithful care. He is my shelter. There is nothing but goodness in him!"

OT *Ezekiel 34:16:* "I will seek my lost ones, those who strayed away, and bring them safely home again. I will put

splints and bandages upon their broken limbs and heal the
sick."

OT   *Psalm 103:10–12:* "He has not punished us as we deserve
for all our sins, for his mercy toward those who fear and
honor him is as great as the height of the heavens above
the earth. He has removed our sins as far away from us as
the east is from the west."

OT   *Psalm 91:10–11:* "How then can evil overtake me or any
plague come near? For he orders his angels to protect you
wherever you go."

OT   *Psalm 91:3–4:* "For he rescues you from every trap, and
protects you from the fatal plague. He will shield you
with his wings! They will shelter you. His faithful promises are your armor."

OT   *Psalm 84:6:* "When they walk through the Valley of Weeping it will become a place of springs where pools of
blessing and refreshment collect after rains!"

OT   *Jeremiah 29:11–13:* "For I know the plans I have for you,
says the Lord. They are plans for good and not for evil, to
give you a future and a hope. In those days when you
pray, I will listen. You will find me when you seek me, if
you look for me in earnest."

OT   *Zechariah 2:8:* "The Lord of Glory has sent me [this is believed to be the Messiah speaking] against the nations that
oppressed you, for he who harms you sticks his finger in
Jehovah's eye!"

Please note that all of the above Scriptures are from the
Old Testament. I just wanted you to see that the believers
then knew the same loving God that believers today know.
And now a few New Testament references.

Romans 11:33–34: "Oh, what a wonderful God we have!
How great are his wisdom and knowledge and riches!
How impossible it is for us to understand his decisions
and his methods! For who among us can know the mind
of the Lord?"

2 Corinthians 1:3: "What a wonderful God we have—he is
the Father of our Lord Jesus Christ, the source of every
mercy, and the one who so wonderfully comforts and
strengthens us in our hardship and trials. And why does
he do this? So that when others are troubled, needing our

sympathy and encouragement, we can pass on to them this same help and comfort God has given us."

Heavenly Father, we just bow before you, overwhelmed by your love for your children. Thank you for your expression of this love in your Word. Thank you for loving us. In your precious Son's name. Amen.

What about Those Who Never Hear about Jesus Christ?

THE SUBJECT OF this chapter is one of the big hang-ups in the nonbelieving world today regarding Christianity. I wish I had some easy answers for you, but I don't. . . .

Romans 11:34: "*For who among us can know the mind of the Lord?* Who knows enough to be his counselor and guide?"

. . . What I *do* have is a profound sense of *Who* God is. One of His attributes is righteousness—perfectness. Thus, I know that God is upright in character—faithful, just, and equitable. I also know from this that God does not lie!

Titus 1:2: "In hope of eternal life, which God, *that cannot lie,* promised before the world began" (KJV).

Okay! I know he cannot lie and I know that he has promised that those who sincerely seek him will find him.

OT *Jeremiah 29:13:* "*You will find me when you seek me, if you look for me in earnest.*"

Luke 11:10: "Everyone who asks, receives; *all who seek, find;* and the door is opened to everyone who knocks."

God does not break his promises. . . .

Romans 4:21: ". . . that God was well able to do anything he promised."

2 Corinthians 1:20: "He [Jesus] carries out and fulfills all of God's promises, no matter how many of them there are. . . ."

God has also promised that the Truth is revealed to *all* men.

John 1:6–9: "There was a man sent from God, whose name was John. The same came for a witness, to bear witness of the Light [Jesus], that all men through him might believe. He was not that Light, but was sent to bear witness of that Light. *That was the true Light, which lighteth every man that cometh into the world"* (KJV).

Romans 1:17-20: "This Good News tells us that God makes us ready for heaven—makes us right in God's sight—when we put our faith and trust in Christ to save us. This is accomplished from start to finish by faith. As the Scripture says it, 'The man who finds life will find it through trusting God.' But God shows his anger from heaven against all sinful, evil men who push away the truth from them. *For the truth about God is known to them instinctively; God has put this knowledge in their hearts.* Since earliest times men have seen the earth and sky and all God made, and have known of his existence and great eternal power. So they will have no excuse [when they stand before God at Judgment Day]" [brackets in Scripture not mine].

This is really God's business when we stick our noses into the problem about those who never "hear" about Jesus Christ. God has promised that those who earnestly seek him will find him! And I believe he is "well able to do anything he promises." So let's leave those folks in God's hands. Let's worry about those who *aren't* genuinely seeking him! The world is full of people like that! This isn't true just today! This has been true from the beginning! I choose to believe in the Creator's mercy and love for his creatures and I choose to believe what Jesus Christ said:

John 14:6: ". . . I am the Way—yes, and the Truth and the Life. *No one can get to the Father except by means of me."*

Christ also said he was God! (So I know he cannot lie either.)

John 10:30: "I and my Father are one" (KJV).

John 8:24: ". . . unless you believe that *I am the Messiah, the Son of God,* you will die in your sins."

John 14:9: ". . . Anyone who has seen me has seen the Father! . . ."

I believe! And I will not be "lost" worrying about God's business. He is well able to tend to it!

It all comes back to F-A-I-T-H! This is beautifully expressed in the Old Testament:

OT   *Habakkuk 2:4:* "Note this: Wicked men [nonbelievers] trust
      themselves alone, and fail; but *the righteous man [be-*
      liever] trusts in me, and lives!"
      . . . and in the New Testament:
      Romans 1:17: ". . . *This is accomplished from **start to**
      finish by faith. As the Scripture says it, 'The man who
      finds life will find it through trusting God.'"
Let the Creator worry about his creatures! You will discover through studying about the Lord that he loves his
creatures far more than you do.
      2 Peter 3:9: "He isn't really being slow about his promised
      return [second coming], even though it sometimes seems
      that way. But he is waiting, for the good reason that *he is*
      not willing that any should perish, and he is giving more
      time for sinners [all over the world] to repent."
Work on your personal relationship with Him . . . grow
strong in the Lord . . . and you will then have a great deal
to share with the "lost sheep" of the world. In doing this you
will be helping tell the world about Jesus Christ.
      In addition to the question "What Happens to Those
Who Never Hear about Jesus?" there is a closely related
question that comes up frequently about infants and little
children who die before they have a chance to know Jesus
Christ—"the innocents."
      Matthew 18:10: "See that you do not look down on one of
      these little ones. For I tell you that *their angels in heaven*
      always see the face of my Father in heaven" (NIV).
      Matthew 19:14: "Jesus said, 'Let the little children come to
      me, and do not hinder them, for *the Kingdom of heaven*
      belongs to such as these'" (NIV).
      Matthew 18:14: "In the same way *your Father in heaven is*
      not willing that any of these little ones should be lost"
      (NIV).
In the above verses you can see how very special little
children are to the Lord, but the one which perfectly expresses, to me, God's love for little children is:
OT   *Isaiah 40:11:* "He tends His flock like a shepherd: *He*
      *gathers the lambs [little children] in His arms and **carries**
      them close to His heart; He gently leads those that have
      young" (NIV).

Little children are really special to God. He carries them! There is no specific "age of accountability" ever mentioned in the Bible, and I believe this is intentional on God's part. He created each one of us as a unique creature. The age of accountability is, therefore, unique to each creature.

We have now come full circle on this question. It still gets back to a profound sense of who God is . . . and he is wonderful!

OT   *Isaiah 9:6:* "For unto us a Child is born; unto us a Son is given; and the government shall be upon his shoulder. These will be his royal titles: 'Wonderful,' 'Counselor,' 'The Mighty God,' 'The Everlasting Father,' 'The Prince of Peace.' "

Dear heavenly Father, thank you for your Son, Jesus Christ, who would have died for me even if I was the only person on the earth. Your unconditional love just amazes me. Oh, Lord, give me a sense of what that kind of love really means and enable me more each day, Father, to love my brothers and sisters in this way. In Jesus' name. Amen.

WHAT IS IT WE REALLY WANT?

1. We All Want Security
2. Jesus Christ—The Only Real Security
3. How Do I Get This Security?
4. You Still Have Not Told Me How I Get This Security!

We All Want Security

EVERYONE IS interested in and searching for security in this life. For many, the search is frustrating and endless. Why? Because they are looking in all the wrong places. Is there any real security in the things of this world?

Matthew 6:19–21: "Don't store up treasures here on earth where they can erode away or may be stolen. Store them in heaven where they will never lose their value, and are safe from thieves. *If your profits are in heaven your heart will be there too.*"

Matthew 6:24: "You cannot serve two masters: God and money. For you will hate one and love the other, or else the other way around."

1 Timothy 6:7: "After all, we didn't bring any money with us when we came into the world, and we can't carry away a single penny when we die."

Let's have a look at what Webster's Dictionary says about security. First, it says it is a noun. The definitions are as follows: 1) *the quality or state of being secure; as* (a) *freedom from danger; safety;* (b) *freedom from fear or anxiety;* 2) (a) something given, deposited, or pledged to make certain the fulfillment of an obligation; (b) surety; 3) an evidence of debt or of property (as a stock certificate or bond); 4) (a) *something that secures; protection;* (b) measures taken especially to guard against espionage or sabotage.

After looking over the above, I would say I am definitely looking for 1(a) and (b) and 4(a). Aren't you? The one

that most specifically defines what I view as security is 1(b):
freedom from fear or anxiety. That is security!

(I have learned that the things of this world—wealth,
power, religion, philosophy, intellect, relationships, etc.—
only increased my anxieties and fears . . . and made me
more desperate.

1 Corinthians 3:11: "And *no one can ever lay any other real
foundation* than that one we [Christians] already have—
Jesus Christ.")

This is the real joy of this book . . . because it is about the
only real security we can have and how we get it. That
security is Jesus Christ.

There is an old hymn which reflects perfectly my security.
"Upon the rock of Christ I stand;/Everything else is shifting sand." There is also Scripture which deals with security
in the same way:

Matthew 7:24-27: "All who listen to my instructions and
follow them are wise, like a man who builds his house on
solid rock. Though the rain comes in torrents, and the
floods rise and the storm winds beat against his house, it
won't collapse, for it is built on rock. But those who hear
my instructions and ignore them are foolish, like a man
who builds his house on sand. For when the rains and
floods come, and storm winds beat against his house, it will
fall with a mighty crash."

2 Timothy 2:19: "But God's truth stands firm like a great
rock, and nothing can shake it. It is a foundation
stone. . . ."

Jesus Christ is eternal security. He and he alone has the
power to change lives. Jesus Christ is THE ROCK.

OT   *Psalm 40:2–3:* "He brought me up also out of an horrible
pit, out of the miry clay, *and set my feet upon a rock,*
and established my goings. And he hath put a new song
in my mouth, even praise unto our God: many shall see it,
and fear, and shall trust in the Lord" (KJV).

OT   *Psalm 18:31:* "For who is God, save the Lord? Or who is a
rock, save our God?" (KJV).

Matthew 16:18: ". . . and upon this rock [Jesus] I will
build my church, and the gates of hades shall not prevail
against it."

In Matthew, the Greek word for rock is *petra,* which translates as "a massive rock or boulder; a refuge." That rock never budges, but the minute I choose to step off of it I am into shifting sand! Quick sand! But do you know something beautiful about that rock? As soon as I am ready to step back on it, no matter how far or how long I have strayed from it, it takes but a single step to get back on. It is waiting for me . . . not with condemnation but with love.

OT *Deuteronomy 32:4:* "He is the Rock, his work is perfect: for all his ways are judgment: a God of truth and without iniquity, just and right is he" (KJV).

Wouldn't you like to know more about the Rock?

Are you taking it nice and easy on your studies? You didn't get to know your best friend in a day, or a week or even in a month. You cannot possibly absorb the wonder and beauty of God in his Word by sitting down and breezing through this book. Take your time. There's plenty more when you finish this book!

Dear, sweet heavenly Father, we thank you for the wonder and beauty of your Word. Oh, Lord, teach your little ones what you want them to know and help them to understand what you want them to understand . . . and Father, move them at your pace. In Christ's name we pray. Amen.

Jesus Christ—The Only Real Security

THE SECURITY OF Jesus Christ is the promise of eternal life with God, the Father, Son and Holy Spirit. The other alternative is eternal life with Satan in hell. Frankly, that alternative does not make me feel very secure. Does it you? The neat thing about eternal life with God is that it begins the moment you receive Christ as your personal Lord and Savior. You don't have to wait for your body to die physically to be united with God. The security of Jesus Christ and eternal life is also manifested to me through the consistency and constancy of God himself, the steadfastness of his personality and character and his faithfulness to his Word.

John 11:25–26: "Jesus told her, 'I am the one who raises the dead [from sin] and gives them life again. *Anyone who believes in me, though he dies like anyone else [physically], shall live again.* He is given eternal life for believing in me and shall never perish. Do you believe this. . . .'"

1 John 5:11–12: "And *what is it that God has said? That he has given us eternal life, and that this life is in his Son.* So whoever has God's Son has life, whoever does not have his Son, does not have life."

The above two Scriptures say very clearly the essence of the Gospel (the Good News). The following Scriptures are a beautiful picture of what God did for us. They deserve special time and attention.

John 15:13–14: "And here is how to measure it—*the greatest love is shown when a person lays down his life for his friends; and you are my friends if you obey me."*

Romans 5:7–8: "Even if we were good, we really wouldn't expect anyone to die for us, though, of course, that might be barely possible. *But God showed his great love for us by sending Christ to die for us while we were still sinners."*

John 3:16–18: *"For God so loved the world, that he gave his only begotten Son, that whosoever believeth in him should not perish, but have everlasting life.* For God sent not his Son into the world to condemn the world, but that the world through him might be saved. He that believeth on him is not condemned; but he that believeth not is condemned already, because he hath not believed in the name of the only begotten Son of God" (KJV).

Throughout Scripture, God paints with broad and brilliant brushstrokes a beautiful picture of his consistency and constancy. One of the common threads that I have found is his view of himself as the Shepherd and his people as his sheep. In this next sequence of Scriptures you will be able to see the Good Shepherd's overwhelming love for his sheep —so much love . . . and so powerful . . . and faithful.

OT **Ezekiel 34:11–12:** "For the Lord God says: I will search and find my sheep. I will be like a shepherd looking for his flock. I will find my sheep and rescue them from all the places they were scattered in that dark and cloudy day.

OT **Ezekiel 34:15–16:** "I myself will be the shepherd of my sheep, and cause them to lie down in peace, the Lord God says. I will seek my lost ones, those who strayed away, and bring them safely home again. I will put splints and bandages upon their broken limbs and heal the sick. . . ."

OT **Isaiah 40:11:** "He tends his flock like a shepherd:/He gathers the lambs in his arms/and carries them close to his heart;/he gently leads those that have young" (NIV).

OT **Psalm 23:1:** "The Lord is my Shepherd, I shall not want" (KJV).

At this moment, I would like to return to—

John 15:13–14: "And here is how to measure it—*the greatest love is shown when a person lays down his life for his friends;* and you are my [Jesus'] friends if you obey me." . . . And now we see that the Good Shepherd *did* lay down His life for His sheep.

John 10:11: "*I am the Good Shepherd. The Good Shepherd lays down his life for the sheep.*"

John 10:28: "*And I give unto them eternal life;* and they shall never perish, neither shall any man pluck them out of my hand" (KJV).

Yes . . . the above Scriptures show us that God, through his Son Jesus Christ, came to lay down his life for his sheep. Jesus Christ *is* the Good Shepherd.

The above Scriptures show us also that God's character is unchanging. Old Testament or New, he is the same.

Hebrews 13:8: "Jesus Christ, the same yesterday, and today, and forever" (KJV).

Hebrews 13:5: ". . . I will never leave thee, nor forsake thee" (KJV).

Matthew 28:20: ". . . I am with you always, even to the end of the world."

Hebrews 6:18–20: "He [Christ] has given us both his promise and his oath, two things we can completely count on, for it is impossible for God to tell a lie. Now all those who flee to him to save them can take new courage when they hear such assurances from God; now they can know without doubt that he will give them the salvation that he has promised them. This *certain hope* of being saved is a strong and trustworthy anchor for our souls, connecting us with God himself behind the sacred curtains of heaven, where Christ has gone ahead to plead for us from his position as our High Priest. . . ."

Now that we have had a look at the rock—the basis for our security—let's see how we can claim that security for ourselves . . . how we can make that real in our personal lives.

Good Shepherd, this little sheep gives praise and thanks for your perfect love. Thank you, Good Shepherd, for laying down your life for me. Thank you for giving me the only real security I have ever known or could ever know. Good Shepherd, plant the seeds of hope in the hearts of the little sheep reading this book and encourage him or her to continue, to press onward that he or she might know the "peace that passes all understanding"—eternal security. In your name, Good Shepherd, we pray. Amen.

How Do I Get This Security?

SALVATION—eternal life with God—is a free gift from God to anyone who will receive that gift. The gift is the life, death and resurrection of Jesus Christ. We receive that gift by faith—by believing—that it is ours and by claiming it as ours.

Ephesians 2:8-9: "For by grace are ye saved *through faith;* and that not of yourselves, *it is the gift of God* . . ." (KJV).

Romans 6:23: "For the wages of sin is death, but *the free gift of God is eternal life through Jesus Christ our Lord.*"

(It's so simple! Yet the human mind somehow wants to make it so complicated!

2 Corinthians 11:3: "But I fear, lest by any means, as the serpent beguiled Eve through his subtilty, so your minds should be corrupted from *the simplicity that is in Christ*" (KJV).

You love *your* children! Don't you like to try to make life as easy as possible for them? As parents, it is possible to understand both God's perspective and the rebellious child's perspective.

Matthew 7:11: "If ye then, being evil, know how to give good gifts unto your children, how much more shall your Father which is in heaven give good things to them that ask him?" (KJV).

BY FAITH:

Romans 10:17: "Yet faith comes from listening to this Good News—the Good News about Christ."

Hebrews 11:1: *"What is faith?* It is the confident assurance that something we want is going to happen. It is the certainty that what we hope for is waiting for us, even though we cannot see it up ahead."

Romans 8:24: "We are saved by trusting [having faith]. And *trusting means looking forward to getting something we don't yet have*—for a man who already has something doesn't need to hope and trust that he will get it."

Hebrews 11:6: *"You can never please God without faith,* without depending on him. Anyone who wants to come to God must believe that there is a God and that he rewards those who sincerely look for him."

Romans 3:20–26: "Now do you see it? No one can ever be made right in God's sight by doing what the law commands. For the more we know of God's laws, the clearer it becomes that we aren't obeying them; his laws serve only to make us see that we are sinners.

But now God has shown us a different way to heaven— *not by 'being good enough'* and trying to keep his laws, but by a new way (though not new, really, for the Scriptures told about it long ago). Now God says he will accept and acquit us—declare us 'not guilty'—*if we trust [have faith in]* Jesus Christ to take away our sins. And we all can be saved in this way, by coming to Christ, no matter who we are or what we have been like. Yes, all have sinned; all fall short of God's glorious ideal; yet now God declares us 'not guilty' of offending him *if we trust [have faith]* in Jesus Christ, who in his kindness freely takes away our sins.

For God sent Christ Jesus to take the punishment for our sins and to end all God's anger against us. *He used Christ's blood and our faith* as the means of saving us from his wrath. In this way he was being entirely fair, even though he did not punish those who sinned in former times. For he was looking forward to the time when Christ would come and take away those sins. And now in these days also he can receive sinners in this same way, because Jesus took away their sins. But isn't this unfair for God to let criminals go free, and say that they are innocent? No, for he does it on the basis of their *trust [faith] in Jesus* who took away their sins."

Philippians 3:9: "And become one with him, no longer
counting on being saved by being good enough or by
obeying God's laws, but by trusting [having faith in]
Christ to save me; for *God's way of making us right with
himself depends on faith—counting on Christ alone.*"

Because God is God and is unfathomable, Jesus Christ ex-
horted us many times throughout his ministry to have the
faith of a child.

Matthew 18:3: "And said, Verily I say unto you, Except ye
be converted, and *become as little children,* ye shall not
enter into the Kingdom of Heaven" (KJV).

Luke 18:17: "Verily, I say unto you, whosoever shall not receive the Kingdom of God *like a child* shall in no way
enter it" (KJV).

Matthew 19:14: "But Jesus said, *Permit little children,* and
forbid them not, to come unto me; *for of such is the
Kingdom of Heaven*" (KJV).

Why? Why did Jesus exhort us to have this childlike kind
of faith? Well, I believe he knew that man's mind would
endeavor to intellectualize about him . . . to know all
about him. After all, this is exactly how Adam and Eve fell
from grace in the Garden of Eden. (Later, in the chapter
entitled "How Did We Get into This Mess?" we will go into
this study, but for now, let me briefly explain that Satan first
tempted Eve to eat from the tree of the knowledge of good
and evil by convincing her that she could then know what
God knows.)

OT   *Genesis 3:5:* [This is Satan speaking here] "For God doth
know that in the day ye eat thereof, then your eyes shall
be opened, and *ye shall be as God, knowing good and
evil*" (KJV).

See! We humans have always thought, at least subcon-
sciously, that we could understand the mind of God . . .
but we can't.

Romans 11:33–34: "Oh, what a wonderful God we have!
How great are his wisdom and knowledge and riches!
*How impossible it is for us to understand his decisions and
his methods! For who among us can know the mind of
the Lord?*"

OT   *Isaiah 55:8:* "For my thoughts are not your thoughts, neither
are your ways my ways, saith the Lord" (KJV).

God also warns us that the more we try to intellectualize him, the more confused we will get. Not because he is unjust, but because he wants us to accept him by faith.

Matthew 11:25: "And Jesus prayed this prayer: 'O Father, Lord of heaven and earth, thank you for hiding the truth from those who think themselves so wise, and for revealing it to little children.'"

1 Corinthians 1:27: "Instead, God has deliberately chosen to use ideas the world considers foolish and of little worth in order to shame those people considered by the world as wise and great."

(Why? Because God wants us to look to him, not to man, for our spiritual answers.)

1 Corinthians 2:14: "But the man who isn't a Christian can't understand and can't accept these thoughts from God, which the Holy Spirit teaches us. They sound foolish to him, because only those who have the Holy Spirit within them can understand what the Holy Spirit means. Others just can't take it in."

1 Corinthians 1:25: "This so-called 'foolish' plan of God is far wiser than the wisest plan of the wisest man, and God in his weakness—Christ dying on the cross—is far stronger than any man."

NOT BY WORKS (GOOD DEEDS—BEING GOOD ENOUGH):

Salvation is a gift. That's what we have just looked at in the previous section. We cannot earn salvation through "being good enough."

Ephesians 2:8–9: "Because of his kindness you have been saved through trusting Christ. And even trusting is not of yourselves; it too is a gift from God. *Salvation is not a reward for the good we have done,* so none of us can take any credit for it."

Romans 10:3–4: "For they don't understand that Christ has died to make them right with God. *Instead they are trying to make themselves good enough to gain God's favor by keeping the Jewish laws and customs, but that is not God's way of salvation.* They don't understand that Christ gives to those who trust him everything they are trying to get by keeping his laws. He ends all of that."

Romans 11:6: "And if it is by God's kindness, then *it is not by their being good enough.* For in that case the free gift would no longer be free—it isn't free when it is earned." Satan loves to tell us that if we try hard enough we might be good enough to go to heaven when we die, knowing full well that he is tripping us up all day long! But God clearly states right here that it is not by our good deeds (works), or by being a good person that we are saved. The same verses give us the answer. It is by grace *through faith* and is a gift from God.

Okay! I am not saying we should not do good deeds! I am saying that good deeds will not save us. Good works will not bring salvation. Salvation will bring forth good works! Good works will not produce faith. Faith will produce good works!

What I am trying to say is that once we become God's children (through faith), we will have a strong desire to show our God-given love for man by doing for others, motivated by the right desires of our hearts—our love for God.

OT   *Ezekiel 36:26:* "And I will give you a new heart—*I will give you new and right desires*—and put a new spirit within you. . . ."

Though we cannot earn our salvation through our good deeds, God promises that our good deeds—the pouring out of our hearts of the love he has given us—will be rewarded with crowns when we get to heaven.

2 Timothy 4:7–8: "I have fought long and hard for my Lord, and through it all I have kept true to him. And now the time has come for me to stop fighting and rest. *In heaven a crown is waiting for me* which the Lord, the righteous Judge, will give me on that great day of his return. And not just to me, but to all those whose lives show that they are eagerly looking forward to his coming back again."

Revelation 22:12: " 'See, I [Jesus] am coming soon, and my reward is with me, *to repay everyone according to the deeds he has done.*' "

I pray you are going slowly. Your head may be able to take this in quickly, but your heart needs time to absorb . . . and faith is a matter of the heart—not the head!

Almighty and everlasting God, thank you for the gift of faith. Thank you for the gift of eternal life. Lord, I pray that the one reading this book and learning through your Word to know you is really experiencing a heart understanding, not just intellectual knowledge. For it is in Christ's name that we pray. Amen.

You Still Have Not Told Me How I Get This Security!

MANY OF YOU have already invited Jesus Christ into your life, but for the benefit of those who have not yet chosen Christ as Lord and Savior, let's go over it in a clear way. *God wants you to choose to believe in him.* He nudges us and lets us know he is there, but we still must choose him. Yes, he could have created us without a choice. But can you, for one minute, visualize yourself pulling the string of one of those dolls that talks and is programmed to say "I love you! I love you!" *Would that make you feel loved?* Neither does God want a programmed kind of love from us. He wants us to love him because we choose to love him. He is waiting.

Revelation 3:20–21: "Look! I have been standing at the door [of your heart] and I am constantly knocking. *If anyone hears me calling him and opens the door, I will come in and fellowship with him and he with me.* I will let every one who conquers sit beside me on my throne, just as I took my place with my Father on his throne when I had conquered."

Here is a vivid picture of Christ himself saying that he is waiting to be invited in. He will not come in unless he is invited. He won't force himself on anyone. He wants you to choose him!

John 3:3: "Jesus replied, 'With all the earnestness I possess I tell you this: *Unless you are born again, you can never get into the Kingdom of God.*'"

Christ is saying here that the born-again experience is a spiritual one. Just as we are born physically . . . so we must also be born spiritually. A beautiful example of this in nature is the butterfly. The caterpillar wraps itself in a cocoon. After a period of dormancy, it emerges a beautiful butterfly. The butterfly is symbolic of Christ's death, burial, and resurrection. The rebirth!

John 14:23: "Jesus replied, 'Because I will only reveal myself to those who love me and obey me. *The Father will love them too, and we will come to them and live with them.'*"

Here Jesus says that if we love him and choose him, he and the Father will come to live inside us. In Galatians 2:20, Paul said that it was Christ who lived within him.

1 Corinthians 6:19: "Haven't you yet learned that your body is the home of the Holy Spirit God gave you, and that *he lives within you?* Your own body does not belong to you."

Once more, we see that God, the Holy Spirit, lives inside us. God the Father, Son and Holy Spirit, lives inside us!

Romans 6:23: "For the wages of sin is death, but *the free gift of God is eternal life through Jesus Christ our Lord.*"

Luke 11:10: "*Everyone who asks, receives;* all who seek, find; and the door is opened to everyone who knocks."

Receive the free gift of eternal life through Jesus Christ.

If you have never invited Jesus Christ into your life and you would like to do so, a very simple prayer is all that is necessary. You might try something like this:

Lord Jesus, I confess that I am a sinner and that I need you. I confess that I do not know you . . . but I would like to know you. Therefore, by faith, I invite you, Lord Jesus, into my heart to be my Lord and Savior. Thank you for dying for my sins and thank you that you promise to come into my life. Teach me what you want me to know and help me to understand through your Holy Spirit what you want me to understand.

If this prayer does not express your desires and feelings, just say it in your own way . . . as if you were talking to your best friend . . . because *you are!*

Just remember one thing. Everyone expects some noticeable change in his or her feelings at this momentous time, but with most people, the feelings come later. Just know that *God does not lie* and that he says if you invite him into your life he *will* come in. Knowing that is faith!

Romans 10:9–10: "For if you tell others with your own mouth that Jesus Christ is your Lord, and believe in your own heart that God has raised him from the dead, you will be saved. For it is by believing in his heart that a man becomes right with God; and with his mouth he tells others of his faith, confirming his salvation."

Tell *someone* . . . your mother . . . your best friend . . . your husband! Telling someone will confirm to you what you have accepted in your heart.

Oh, God, how wonderful that you have already reserved a place in heaven for me. Help me to learn to rest in my faith . . . to lie back in your everlasting arms and let you love me. How I have needed that unconditional love that only you can give. My Lord, my God, how I adore you! I praise you in Jesus' name. Amen.

OKAY, I'VE DONE THIS. WHAT HAPPENS NOW?

1. I Now Know Jesus Christ Personally— He Will Become My Best Friend More Each Day
2. I Am Indwelled by the Holy Spirit
3. The Abundant Life

I Now Know Jesus Christ Personally—
He Will Become My Best Friend
More Each Day

ONCE WE ACCEPT Jesus Christ, the gift of life, he begins to reveal himself to us. I began to notice right away that I did not feel as alone as I had. It was not a sudden, dramatic change, but I did begin to sense that the lonely void inside me was slowly being filled.

The only real way that God can begin to reveal himself in any big way is through studying of his Word. That is why I am excited about this book. In it, I not only hope you can share my feelings and beliefs about Jesus Christ, but also what God has to say about himself. At best, I can be as honest with you as I know how, but that isn't enough. I have a human mind and am susceptible to error. *God's Word can be counted on.* He never makes a mistake.

God's Word tells us over and over again that he knows us personally!

OT   *Psalm 139:* "O Lord, you have examined my heart and know everything about me. You know when I sit or stand. When far away you know my every thought. You chart the path ahead of me, and tell me where to stop and rest. Every moment, you know where I am. You know what I am going to say before I even say it. You both precede and follow me, and place your hand of blessing on my head.

"This is too glorious, too wonderful to believe! I can *never* be lost to your Spirit! I can *never* get away from my God! If I go up to heaven, you are there; if I go down to the place of the dead, you are there. If I ride the morning winds to the farthest oceans, even there your hand will guide me, your strength will support me. If I try to hide in the darkness, the night becomes light around me. For even darkness cannot hide from God; to you the night shines as bright as day. Darkness and light are both alike to you.

"You made all the delicate, inner parts of my body, and knit them together in my mother's womb. Thank you for making me so wonderfully complex! It is amazing to think about. Your workmanship is marvelous—and how well I know it. You were there while I was being formed in utter seclusion! You saw me before I was born and scheduled each day of my life before I began to breathe. Every day was recorded in your Book!

"How precious it is, Lord, to realize that you are thinking about me constantly! I can't even count how many times a day your thoughts turn towards me. And when I waken in the morning, you are still thinking of me!

"Surely you will slay the wicked, Lord! Away, bloodthirsty men! Begone! They blaspheme your name and stand in arrogance against you—how silly can they be? O Lord, shouldn't I hate those who hate you? Shouldn't I be grieved with them? Yes, I hate them, for your enemies are my enemies too.

"Search me, O God, and know my heart; test my thoughts. Point out anything you find in me that makes you sad, and lead me along the path of everlasting life."

OT *Psalm 56:8:* "You have seen me tossing and turning through the night. You have collected all my tears and preserved them in your bottle! You have recorded every one in your book."

OT *Job 31:4:* "He sees everything I do, and every step I take."

OT *Malachi 3:16:* ". . . And he had a Book of Remembrance drawn up in which he recorded the names of those who feared him and loved to think about him."

OT *Isaiah 41:13:* "I am holding you by your right hand—I, the Lord your God—and I say to you, Don't be afraid; I am here to help you."

Matthew 10:30: "And the very hairs of your head are all numbered."

OT *Psalm 23:1:* "The Lord is my shepherd; I shall not want" (KJV).

Hebrews 4:13: "He knows about everyone, everywhere. Everything about us is bare and wide open to the all-seeing eyes of our living God; nothing can be hidden from him to whom we must explain all that we have done."

ot   **Psalm 121:3–4:** "He will never let me stumble, slip or fall. For he is always watching, never sleeping."

ot   **Isaiah 43:2:** "When you go through deep waters and great trouble, I will be with you. When you go through rivers of difficulty, you will not drown! When you walk through the fire of oppression, you will not be burned up—the flames will not consume you."

I bet you didn't know that God knew you that well and loved you that much! Surprise, surprise! Our relationship with him through his Son Jesus Christ is truly one of deep and personal knowledge—we to him and he to us. Oh, how he woos us!

ot   **Song of Solomon 2:8:** "The voice of my beloved [my Savior]! Behold, he cometh leaping upon the mountains, skipping upon the hills" (kjv).

ot   **Song of Solomon 2:10:** "My beloved spoke, and said unto me, Rise up, my love, my fair one, and come away [with me]" (kjv).

ot   **Song of Solomon 2:16:** "My beloved is mine, and I am his; he feedeth among the lilies" (kjv).

Abba (Daddy), I praise you that you are not only my Father but my best friend as well. What a comfort that you will never leave me nor forsake me. What a comfort that you never sleep and are always watching over me. Thank you . . . in His name. Amen.

I Am Indwelled by the Holy Spirit

John 14:15–17: "If you love me, obey me [Jesus]; and I will ask the Father and he will give you another Comforter, and he will never leave you. He is the Holy Spirit, the Spirit who leads into all truth. The world at large cannot receive him, for it isn't looking for him and doesn't recognize him. But you do, for *he lives with you now and some day shall be in you.*"

(The reason Jesus said he "some day shall be in you" was because Jesus had not yet died and been resurrected. The Holy Spirit did not come until then.

John 16:7: "But the fact of the matter is that *it is best for you that I* [Jesus] go away, for if I don't, the Comforter [the Holy Spirit] won't come. If I do, he will—for I will send him to you.")

Ephesians 1:13: "And because of what Christ did, all you others too, who heard the Good News about how to be saved, and trusted Christ, were marked as belonging to Christ by the Holy Spirit, who long ago had been promised to all of us Christians."

1 Corinthians 6:17: "But he that is joined unto the Lord is one spirit" (KJV).

1 Corinthians 6:19: "Haven't you yet learned that your body is the home of the Holy Spirit God gave you, and that *he lives within you?* Your own body does not belong to you."

The Holy Spirit is given to us by God for many reasons. Let's take a look at them.

He comforts us.

John 14:26: "But when the Father sends the Comforter in-

stead of me—and by the Comforter I mean the Holy
Spirit. . . ."
He pricks our conscience when we commit sin.
*John 16:8: "And when he has come he will convince the
world of its sin, and of the availability of God's goodness,
and of deliverance from judgment."*
He helps us understand the Bible and gives us spiritual wisdom.
1 Corinthians 2:10: ". . . God has sent his Spirit to tell us,
and *his Spirit searches out and shows us all of God's deepest secrets."*
1 John 2:27: "But you have received the Holy Spirit and he
lives within you, in your hearts, so that you don't need
anyone to teach you what is right. *For he teaches you all
things, and he is the Truth,* and no liar; and so, just as he
has said, you must live in Christ, never to depart from
him."
John 16:13: "When the Holy Spirit, who is truth, comes, *he
shall guide you into all truth,* for he will not be presenting
his own ideas, but will be passing on to you what he has
heard. He will tell you about the future."

OT *Isaiah 11:2:* "And the Spirit of the Lord shall rest upon him,
*the Spirit of wisdom, understanding, counsel and might;
the Spirit of knowledge and of the fear of the Lord."*
(We can also see from the above four Scriptures that God
actually speaks to us through his Holy Spirit. Throughout
time, few men have actually heard the voice of God, but all
Christians, through an "inner ear," hear God speaking to
them.)
1 Corinthians 2:16: ". . . But, strange as it seems, we Christians actually do have within us a portion of the very
thoughts and mind of Christ."
Wow! We are let in on God's deepest secrets! . . . We are
given the mind of Christ!
1 Corinthians 2:15–16: "But the spiritual man has insight
into everything, and that bothers and baffles the man of
the world [the nonbeliever], who can't understand him at
all. How could he? For certainly he has never been one to
know the Lord's thoughts, or to discuss them with him, or
to move the hands of God by prayer. But, strange as it

seems, we Christians actually do have within us a portion of the very thoughts and mind of Christ."

What a gift of God!!!

The Holy Spirit makes us feel good about ourselves and everything else.

Romans 14:17: "For, after all, the important thing for us as Christians is not what we eat or drink but stirring up goodness and peace and joy *from the Holy Spirit.*"

Romans 5:5: "Then, when that happens, we are able to hold our heads high no matter what happens and know that all is well, for we know how dearly God loves us, and we feel this warm love everywhere within us because God has given us the Holy Spirit to fill our hearts with his love."

Galatians 5:22–23: "But when the Holy Spirit controls our lives he will produce this kind of fruit in us: love, joy, peace, patience, kindness, goodness, faithfulness, gentleness and self-control. . . ."

He keeps us from being "slaves" to sin.

James 4:5–6: "Or what do you think the Scripture means when it says that the Holy Spirit, whom God has placed within us, watches over us with tender jealousy? But he gives us more and more strength to stand against all such evil longings. As the Scripture says, God gives strength to the humble, but sets himself against the proud and haughty."

He will help us to memorize Scripture and bring it back to us when we need it.

John 14:26: "But the Comforter, which is the Holy Ghost, whom the Father will send in my name, he shall teach you all things, and *bring all things to your remembrance,* whatsoever I have said unto you" (KJV).

He intercedes with God the Father in our behalf in times of need.

Romans 8:26–27: "And in the same way—by our faith—the Holy Spirit helps us with our daily problems and in our praying. For we don't even know what we should pray for, nor how to pray as we should; but *the Holy Spirit prays for us with such feeling that it cannot be expressed in words.*"

I shall never forget a very deep experience I had which

evidenced this truth to me in a mighty way. From February 1978 to October 1978, I went through some very profound but painful growth in my Christian walk with the Lord. It involved many things—giving up more of *my* ideas, *my* dreams, my old hurts which often came back to haunt me. Late in September, I went into a downward spiral of depression, hopelessness, and despair which was as deep as I have ever been in. Even the day-to-day, normal pressures of life were too much for me and I so wanted to give up.

It was in the blackest, loneliest caverns of my thirty-eight years that one more problem, which seemed insurmountable at the time, popped up. I shall never forget that day as long as I live. As I was taking a shower, I cried out to the Lord in my agony. "Lord God! Am I going to have to go through this alone too?" Not really a prayer! In fact. It was more of a complaint! And yet, in the next days of my life God demonstrated in a powerful way that he heard me.

That night I went to bed as usual. About 2:30 A.M. I awakened (which had become a normal occurrence in my life) and began to pray. But this night a change took place, I felt released, and I returned to the restful sleep of the Lord. The next morning, the telephone rang about 10:00 A.M. It was a girl I had met briefly and visited with on the phone a few times. She said, "Hi, Anne. How are you?" With my habitual compulsion to "cover up," I replied, "Fine." "Are you really?" she queried. And I confessed to her at that moment that all had not been well with me. She said, "Aha! That explains it. The Lord has had your face before me for two weeks. I have been in deep prayer for you. But last night, I awoke and began to intercede for you with great weeping to the Lord as never before(!) But as I prayed," she continued, "a peace came over me, and I got the distinct impression that there had been a change." She had awakened at 1:30 A.M., an hour before I had!

Well, I thanked her for her love and prayers and proceeded with my day. The following Monday was a holiday and there was no mail delivered, but on Tuesday, I received a letter in the mail which read, "Dear Mrs. Murchison, You don't really know me, and I don't know what you are going through, but the Lord has had you in my prayers, literally in tears, for two weeks. I just wanted you to know that I love you and am praying for you."

Are you beginning to get the picture? It certainly took *me* long enough! I fell on my knees in gratitude to my tender, caring Lord, who reached down and touched me through two of his children and said, "No, Anne. You will never ever have to go through anything alone again as long as you live."

Later that week I received a third touch from the Lord. Another friend called and said, "Are you okay?" At this point, I had given up trying to cover up. "I'm great now, but the past few weeks have been hell on earth for me." She said, "I thought so! You have been in my thoughts and prayers almost constantly for the last few weeks. Will you forgive me for not calling you sooner?" Well, what could I say?

This experience was one of the most powerful demonstrations of a loving God who cares deeply about each of his children, and responds personally to our needs that I have ever seen, much less experienced. And I have never been the same. I am so aware of his presence now. I wish so very much I could write it in the magnitude that I experienced it, but there is just no way to express it in a way that would convey to you the power of it. But I believe with all my heart that if you stay close to him, you will be touched by him in a similar but unique way.

This is a picture-perfect example of the Holy Spirit interceding in behalf of God's children.

(By the way, I'd like to share with you that this experience occurred to me very early in the writing of this book and has only been inserted as part of the book as it was about to go to print. Great growth comes from great pain and since the Christian experience is a growing experience, it is painful at times, but, as I said earlier, through Jesus Christ, our problems and pain are but stepping stones to victories.)

Yes, the Holy Spirit is the one who enables us to do things that we are, with our human hearts, unable to do. One of the most profound ways he has manifested this in me is through enabling me to forgive others when I was deeply hurt. What a relief not to have to carry *that* load anymore!

John 14:16–17: "And I will ask the Father and he will give you another Comforter, and he will never leave you. He is the Holy Spirit. . . ."

Romans 8:26: ". . . the Holy Spirit helps us with our daily problems. . . ."

He gives us the words to speak (and write).

Matthew 10:20: "For it won't be you doing the talking—*it will be the Spirit of your heavenly Father speaking through you!*"

This is especially true when witnessing about his Son, Jesus Christ. The Holy Spirit gave me the words for this book, for my testimony, for the teaching. He enables preachers to preach, speakers to speak, teachers to teach . . . and on, and on, and on. *Especially* he enables his children to witness through their lives and their words about Jesus Christ.

Acts 1:8: "But when the Holy Spirit has come upon you, *you will receive power to testify about me* [*Jesus*] **with great effect,** to the people in Jerusalem, throughout Judea, in Samaria, and *to the ends of the earth,* about my death and resurrection."

All of these things are available to you who have received the gift of life through Jesus Christ, our Lord and Savior. But I have saved the best for last!

Romans 5:5: ". . . for we know how dearly God loves us, and we feel this warm love everywhere within us because *God has given us the Holy Spirit to fill our hearts with his love.*"

You are in the process of doing the most important thing you will ever do in your entire life once you have accepted Jesus Christ . . . you are getting to know God! . . . And the more you know about God the more you will be able to trust him. Are you taking the time to absorb and to listen with your "inner ear?"

Heavenly Father, thank you for the gift of the Holy Spirit. Oh, Lord, help us to be sensitive to him. Teach us to listen and to hear. Your riches and your blessings are too wondrous for us to comprehend. Thank you and praise your Holy Name. In Jesus' name we pray.

The Abundant Life

THE ABUNDANT LIFE also begins when we accept Christ and *allow the Holy Spirit to take control of our lives.* It is possible to be a Christian and not live a Spirit-controlled life (the Bible calls this "walking in the Spirit"), so we will study this in greater depth in the next chapter, entitled "What Does God Require of Me?"

The abundant life, one of God's many bonuses to his children, is not always a life filled with the things of the world. The abundant life is, however, an abundance of *God's* riches —love, joy, peace, long-suffering, gentleness, goodness, faith, meekness, self-control and contentment—something all the money and success in the world can't buy. If you don't have all this yet, don't worry. No Christian has them all at all times. It's a lifetime process God takes us through. Journeying through life with Jesus Christ is an exciting adventure. It's not always fun . . . but it's always exciting. Look at it this way. Believer or nonbeliever, life is full of problems, but with Jesus Christ no problem is insurmountable. He uses our problems and pain as stepping stones in our lives! While I am in the middle of problems and pain I may not (and probably won't) see this, but *looking back*, it is always a joy to see what he has done in me and for me!

There are many Scriptures in this section (as there have been in the previous sections), so be patient! It's important to see the goodness and richness of Jesus Christ and the abundant life.

Galatians 5:22: "But when the Holy Spirit controls our lives he will produce this kind of fruit in us: love, joy, peace, patience, kindness, goodness, faithfulness, gentleness and self-control. . . ."

Ephesians 3:20: "Now unto Him Who, by the power that is at work within us, *is able to carry out His purpose and do superabundantly, far over and above all that we dare ask or think—infinitely beyond our highest prayers, desires, thoughts, hopes or dreams . . ."* (*Amplified Bible*).

Hebrews 4:9: "There remaineth therefore *a rest* to the people of God" (KJV).

Philippians 4:11–12: "Not that I was ever in need, for I have learned how to get along happily whether I have much or little. I know how to live on almost nothing or with everything. *I have learned the secret of contentment* in every situation, whether it be a full stomach or hunger, plenty or want."

Philippians 4:7: "If you do this [pray about everything] *you will experience God's peace, which is far more wonderful than the human mind can understand.* His peace will keep your thoughts and your hearts quiet and *at rest* as you trust in Christ Jesus."

John 14:27: "I [Jesus] am leaving you with a gift—*peace of mind and heart! And the peace I give isn't fragile like the peace the world gives.* So don't be troubled or afraid."

2 Corinthians 12:9: "And he said unto me, My grace is sufficient for thee; *for my strength is made perfect in [your] weakness . . ."* (KJV).

Romans 8:28: "And we know that *all things work together for good to them that love God, to them who are called according to his purpose*" (KJV).

Romans 5:3–5: "*We can rejoice, too, when we run into problems and trials for we know that they are good for us— they help us learn to be patient. And patience develops strength of character in us and helps us trust God more each time we use it until finally our hope and faith are strong and steady. Then, when that happens, we are able to hold our heads high no matter what happens and know that all is well, for we know how dearly God loves us, and we feel this warm love everywhere within us because God has given us the Holy Spirit to fill our hearts with his love.*"

Romans 8:38–39: "For I am convinced that *nothing can separate us from his love.* Death can't, and life can't. The angels won't, and all the powers of hell itself cannot keep God's love away. Our fears for today, our worries about tomorrow, or where we are—high above the sky, or in the deepest ocean—nothing will ever be able to separate us from the love of God demonstrated by our Lord Jesus Christ when he died for us."

Hebrews 13:5: ". . . for he hath said, *I will never leave thee, nor forsake thee*" (KJV).

OT *Ecclesiastes 3:14:* "And I know this, that *whatever God does is final*—nothing can be added or taken from it; God's purpose in this is that man should fear [in reverential awe and with a deep sense of accountability] the all-powerful God."

1 Corinthians 2:9: "That is what is meant by the Scriptures which say that *no mere man has ever seen, heard or even imagined what wonderful things God has ready for those who love the Lord.*"

Romans 8:31: "What can we ever say to such wonderful things as these? *If God is on our side, who can ever be against us?*"

OT *Genesis 50:20:* "But as for you, *ye thought evil against me; but God meant it unto good,* to bring to pass, as it is this day, to save much people alive" (KJV).

John 10:10: "The thief's [Satan's] purpose is to steal, kill and destroy. *My purpose is to give life in all its fullness.*"

Matthew 11:28–30: "*Come to me and I will give you rest*—all of you who work so hard beneath a heavy yoke. Wear my yoke—for it fits perfectly—and let me teach you; *for I am gentle and humble, and you shall find rest for your souls;* for I give you only light burdens."

Matthew 6:33: "And *he will give them to you* [*your needs*] *if you give him first place in your life and live as he wants you to.*"

OT *Isaiah 43:2:* "*When you go through deep waters and great trouble, I will be with you.* When you go through rivers of difficulty, you will not drown! When you walk through the fire of oppression, you will not be burned up—the flames will not consume you."

OT   *Psalm 30:5:* "His anger lasts a moment; *his favor lasts for life!* Weeping may go on all night, but in the morning there is joy."

OT   *Psalm 23:1:* *"The Lord is my Shepherd; I shall not want"* (KJV).

OT   *Psalm 139:17–18:* *"How precious it is, Lord, to realize that you are thinking about me constantly!* I can't even count how many times a day your thoughts turn towards me. And when I waken in the morning, you are still thinking of me!"

OT   *Isaiah 54:10:* "For the mountains may depart and the hills disappear, but *my kindness shall not leave you. My promise of peace for you will never be broken,* says the Lord who has mercy upon you."

2 Corinthians 4:17: "These troubles and sufferings of ours are, after all, quite small and won't last very long. Yet this short time of distress will result in God's richest blessing upon us forever and ever!"

Philippians 1:6: "And I am sure that God who began the good work within you will keep right on helping you grow in his grace until his task within you is finally finished on that day when Jesus Christ returns."

OT   *Ezekiel 36:25–27:* "Then it will be as though I had sprinkled clean water on you, for *you will be clean*—your filthiness will be washed away, your idol worship gone. And *I will give you a new heart—I will give you new and right desires—and put a new spirit within you.* I will take out your stony hearts of sin and give you new hearts of love."

1 Peter 1:3–4: "All honor to God, the God and Father of our Lord Jesus Christ; for it is his boundless mercy that has given us the privilege of being born again, so that *we are now members of God's own family.* Now we live in the hope of eternal life because Christ rose again from the dead. And *God has reserved for his children the priceless gift of eternal life;* it is kept in heaven for you, pure and undefiled, beyond the reach of change and decay."

Ephesians 2:5–6: "That even though we were spiritually dead and doomed by our sins, he gave us back our lives again when he raised Christ from the dead—only by his undeserved favor have we ever been saved—and lifted us up from the grave into glory along with Christ, *where we sit with him in the heavenly realms*—all because of what Christ Jesus did."

(Please note that the word *sit* is in the present tense! We can sit—spiritually—with Christ in the heavenly realms *now*. There is a seat in heaven with your name on it!)

I suppose the greatest comfort about the abundant life to me is knowing that God has a perfect plan for the life of each of his children. He is in control, and he will accomplish in each of us that which he desires! I can trust him.

OT *Jeremiah 29:11:* "For I know the plans I have for you, says the Lord. They are plans for good and not for evil, to give you a future and a hope."

God's plans are good plans—the abundant life.

So, we can see from these verses that becoming a Christian does not make us perfect nor does it make life perfect. But we learn to trust that "all things work together for good for those who love God" (Rom. 8:28). The abundant life is peace and joy and contentment, despite what's going on around us.

A good analogy is Noah in the ark. He obeyed God and built the ark (in the middle of the desert) in spite of the harassment and derision of his friends. When the rains came, he was, because of his obedience, safely inside the ark—tossing in the storm—but protected and safe. What happened to his friends?

(Noah's obedience to God is a great example of patience to the believer, because it was a long time between the time God told Noah to build the ark and the time that he told him to enter it. From what I can tell in the Scriptures, it must have been seventy-five or one hundred years. *Seventy-five or one hundred years!* Noah had to put up with all the jeering and hooting that went on all that time! But Noah chose to obey God and not listen to his neighbors and friends. *He believed God!* . . . And he was saved and his neighbors and friends were lost.

Let me encourage you to trust in God as Noah did. Through trusting in him . . . we will receive from him the kind of patience Noah had. God does it for us. All we have to do is trust.)

Patience brings peace, joy and contentment, *whatever* my circumstances. That can come *only* from the Lord!

Patience, peace, joy and contentment *are* the abundant life in Christ.

Almighty and everlasting God, I am totally awe-struck by the beauty of your perfect plan for my life, of your gift of abundant life for all your children. Help us to understand what the abundant life really means . . . and most importantly, help us to learn to live it. In your precious Son's name. Amen.

What Does God Require of Me in Order to Live the Abundant Life?

IN THE PREVIOUS chapter, I mentioned that it is possible to be a Christian without living a Spirit-controlled life (walking in the Spirit). This type of Christian is referred to in Scripture as a carnal Christian.

1 Corinthians 3:3: "For ye are yet carnal: for whereas there is among you envying, and strife, and divisions, are ye not carnal, and walk as men?" (KJV).

1 Corinthians 3:1: "Dear brothers, I have been talking to you as though you were still just babies in the Christian life, who are not following the Lord, but your own desires; I cannot talk to you as I would healthy Christians, who are filled with the Spirit."

Carnal Christians cannot enjoy the abundant life, and the reason is very simple. They are not yielding themselves to the will of God, to his perfect plans for their lives. They are still doing things their way . . . and this is disobedience to God.

This is what it means to be a Spirit-filled Christian—to walk in the Spirit:

Galatians 5:25: "If we are living now by the Holy Spirit's power, *let us follow the Holy Spirit's leading in every part of our lives.*"

Galatians 5:17: "For we naturally love to do evil things that are just the opposite from the things that the Holy Spirit tells us to do; and *the good things we want to do when the Spirit has his way with us are just the opposite of our natural desires. . . .*"

A person walking in the Spirit lives a surrendered life by

trusting in him for the answers. He will give them to us. We can through our "inner ear" learn to hear his voice.

OT **Psalm 16:11:** "Thou wilt shew me the path of life: in thy presense is fullness of joy; at thy right hand there are pleasures for evermore" (KJV).

OT **Proverbs 3:5–8:** *"Trust in the Lord with all thine heart, and lean not unto thine own understanding. In all thy ways acknowledge him, and he shall direct thy paths.* Be not wise in thine own eyes; fear the Lord, and depart from evil. It shall be health to thy navel, and marrow to thy bones" (KJV).

OT **Isaiah 26:3:** *"Thou wilt keep him in perfect peace, whose mind is stayed on thee, because he trusteth in thee.* Trust ye in the Lord forever; for in the Lord is everlasting strength" (KJV).

OT **Psalm 32:8:** *"I [the Lord] will instruct thee and teach thee in the way which thou shalt go;* I will guide thee with mine eye" (KJV).

Romans 12:1–2: "And so, dear brothers, I plead with you to *give your bodies to God. Let them be a living sacrifice, holy—the kind he can accept.* When you think of what he has done for you, is this too much to ask? *Don't copy the behavior and customs of this world, but be a new and different person with a fresh newness in all you do and think.* Then you will learn from your own experience how his ways will satisfy you."

OT **Psalm 37:5:** "Commit everything you do to the Lord. Trust him to help you do it and he will."

OT **Isaiah 58:11:** "And the Lord shall guide thee continually, and satisfy thy soul in drought, and make fat thy bones; and thou shalt be like a watered garden, and like a spring of water, whose waters fail not."

OT **Psalm 5:11:** *"But [Lord] make everyone rejoice who puts his trust in you.* Keep them shouting for joy because you are defending them. Fill all who love you with your happiness."

OT **Psalm 34:8:** "Oh, put God to the test and see how kind he is! See for yourself the way *his mercies shower down on all who trust in him.*"

Hebrews 13:6: ". . . The Lord is my Helper and I am not afraid of anything that mere man can do to me."

Walking in the Spirit is "living pleasing unto God." No one is able to do this perfectly . . . but the longer you walk with him, the more able you will become.

Walking in the Spirit opens the lid to God's treasure chest —the wealth of his riches.

Romans 8:5: "Those who let themselves be controlled by their lower natures live only to please themselves, but *those who follow after the Holy Spirit find themselves doing those things that please God. Following after the Holy Spirit leads to life and peace,* but following after the old nature leads to death."

Galatians 5:22: "But when the Holy Spirit controls our lives he will produce this kind of fruit in us: love, joy, peace, patience, kindness, goodness, faithfulness, gentleness and self-control."

1 Corinthians 13:13: "There are three things that remain— faith, hope, and love—and the greatest of these is love."

What a joy it is to walk in the Spirit! How comforting to walk hand in hand with the Lord!

OT *Isaiah 41:13:* "I am holding you by your right hand—I, the Lord your God—and I say to you, Don't be afraid; I am here to help you."

Sweet heavenly Father, teach us to trust you . . . .to yield to your will for our lives. Make spiritual men and women of us, O Lord. Fill us with your Holy Spirit. For it is in Christ's name that we pray. Amen.

UNDERSTANDING SIN IS UNDERSTANDING ONESELF

1. All Sin Is Against God
2. The Dreaded Word—Sin
3. I Must Accept My Sinful Nature
4. I Have a New Heart
5. God's Righteousness vs. Self-Righteousness —Christ Makes Me Worthy

All Sin Is Against God

GOD SAYS OVER and over in his Word that all sin is against him. Because all sin is against him and therefore separates us from him, it is imperative for us to understand sin. This is always a distasteful subject to nonbelievers and new believers, but in order to understand why I need a Savior—why Jesus had to die for me—I need to understand sin.

David committed adultery with Uriah's wife, Bathsheba, and subsequently murdered him that he might have Bathsheba for himself. *Yet David confessed that his sin was against God—not Uriah!*

OT *Psalm 51:4:* "*It is against you and you alone I sinned, and did this terrible thing.* You saw it all, and your sentence against me is just."

There are many Scriptures which support this.

Matthew 25:40: "And I, the King [Jesus], will tell them 'When you did it to these my brothers *you were doing it to me.*'"

Matthew 25:45: "And I will answer, 'When you refused to help the least of these my brothers, *you were refusing help to me.*'"

Luke 10:16: "*He that heareth you, heareth me; and he that despiseth you, despiseth me; and he that despiseth me, despiseth him that sent me*" (KJV).

This violates what God says is most important to him!

Matthew 22:37–38: "Jesus replied, 'Love the Lord your God with all your heart, soul, and mind. This is the first and greatest commandment.'"

All sin begins because we do not love God first—with all our hearts, souls and minds. All sin is, therefore, against God and separates us from him.

Why does sin separate us from him? Because he is holy— pure and righteous. He cannot look upon anything unclean.

OT *Habakkuk 1:13:* "Thou [God] art of purer eyes than to behold evil, and *canst not look on iniquity* . . ." (KJV).

OT *Isaiah 59:2:* "But the trouble is that *your sins have cut you off from God.* Because of sin he has turned his face away from you and will not listen anymore."

OT *Psalm 66:18:* "If I regard iniquity in my heart, the Lord will not hear me" (KJV).

OT *Jeremiah 5:25:* "Your iniquities have turned away these things, and your sins have withholden good things from you" (KJV).

Because sin separates us from God, it is a very serious matter. That's why we are going to spend a good deal of time on this subject.

My Lord . . . Jesus . . . my Savior! Thank you for your death on the cross for my sins. Thank you that because of your death and resurrection I have been made right in your sight . . . in spite of the fact that I do not always love you with my whole heart, soul and mind. Because of you, I can fellowship with God, the Father, Son, and Holy Spirit, and have a personal relationship with you. There is nothing so wonderful as this! In your name I pray. Amen.

The Dreaded Word—Sin

EVERYONE *thinks* he or she knows what sin is. "Sin" as the world knows it refers to specific iniquities such as gossip, murder, pride, envy, adultery, and many others. It is helpful in understanding sin to replace the words *sin* and *iniquity* with the word *disobedience* (to God). This also puts obedience and disobedience into better perspective.

Using Adam and Eve's sin in the garden as an example, it certainly was not the fruit God was upset about! *It was their disobedience to him.*

In the previous chapter we saw that disobedience begins because we do not love God with our whole hearts, souls and minds. The word *heart* is used well over eight hundred times in the Bible and *love begins in the heart*. Therefore, when we disobey God we are not loving him first; thus disobedience (sin) also begins in our hearts. The condition of the heart is the real problem.

OT   *Proverbs 21:2:* "Every way of a man is right in his own eyes: but *the Lord pondereth the hearts*" (KJV).

Matthew 15:18–19: "But evil words come from an evil heart, and defile the man who says them. For *from the heart* come evil thoughts, murder, adultery, fornication, theft, lying and slander."

OT   *Jeremiah 17:9–10:* "*The heart is the most deceitful thing there is, and desperately wicked.* No one can really know how bad it is! Only the Lord knows! . . ."

". . . No one can really know how bad it is! Only the Lord knows! . . ." He understands our real problem, even if we don't!

It also helps to look at the Greek word for sin, *hamartia,*
which translates simply as "missing the mark."

Missing the mark! . . . I guess we could all say that we
have done that! Ever since Adam and Eve, mankind has been
"missing the mark."

Romans 3:23: "Yes, all have sinned; all fall short of God's
glorious ideal" [all miss the mark].

Romans 14:23: ". . . for *whatever is not of faith is sin*"
(KJV).

OT **Isaiah 53:6:** "*All we like sheep have gone astray; we have
turned every one to his own way* . . ." (KJV).

Shock of all shocks! "Doing our own thing" is a sin! Going
our own way is not loving God first!

The world is full of people who don't believe in sin (because they don't really understand it) and therefore see no
need for a Savior. But God is very clear on this!

1 John 1:8: "If we say that we have no sin, we deceive ourselves, and the truth is not in us" (KJV).

The world is also full of people who see themselves as *too*
sinful (or who don't really understand sin) and therefore
carry a heavy burden of guilt around with them. God is very
clear on this too. Neither one of these schools of thought is
correct!

It's astounding to nonbelievers and new believers (and it
certainly was to me) that God views no one sin as greater
than another . . . thus no sinner as worse than another. Disobedience is just that to God . . . disobedience. Yes, that
goes for murder and apples (in the Garden of Eden) too.
Let's take a look.

James 2:10: "*And the person who keeps every law of God,
but makes one little slip, is just as guilty* as the person who
has broken every law there is."

Matthew 5:21–22: "Under the law of Moses the rule was, 'If
you kill, you must die.' But I have added to that rule, and
tell you that if you are only angry, even in your own home,
you are in danger of judgment! If you call your friend an
idiot, you are in danger of being brought before the court.
And if you curse him, you are in danger of the fires of
hell."

1 John: 3:15: "Anyone who hates his Christian brother is really a murderer *at heart;* and you know that no one wanting to murder has eternal life *within.*"

Here, once again, in this verse, we see the heart attitude being examined and judged.

The above verses show that *all* are sinners in God's eyes and *one is not more sinful than another.* We're all equal as sinners and that is why God tells us not to judge others.

Matthew 7:1–3: "Don't criticize, and then you won't be criticized. For others will treat you as you treat them. And *why worry about a speck in the eye of a brother when you have a board in your own?*"

This entire chapter can be summarized very easily. God does not judge us regarding salvation according to what we do, or do not do—because he sees us all as sinners. He judges us according to what his Son, Jesus Christ, did—and whether or not we accept him.

Ephesians 2:8–9: "Because of his kindness *you have been saved through trusting Christ.* And even trusting is not of yourselves; it too is a gift from God. *Salvation is not a reward for the good we have done,* so none of us can take any credit for it."

John 8:24: ". . . for *unless you believe* that I am the Messiah, the Son of God, *you will die in your sins.*"

Romans 1:18: "But God shows his anger from heaven against all sinful, evil men who push away the truth from them."

(Jesus said, "I am the Truth" [*John 14:6*].)

Romans 2:8: "But he will terribly punish those who *fight against the truth of God* and walk in evil ways [those who don't believe]—God's anger will be poured out upon them."

And yet we see how patient and long-suffering God is to his children. The thief who was crucified at the same time Jesus was, was saved "through faith" as he was dying.

Luke 23:39–43: "One of the criminals hanging beside him scoffed, 'So you're the Messiah, are you? Prove it by saving yourself—and us, too, while you're at it!' *But the other criminal protested, 'Don't you even fear God when you are dying?* We deserve to die for our evil deeds, but this man [Jesus] hasn't done one thing wrong.' Then he said, '*Jesus, remember me* when you come into your Kingdom.' *And*

Jesus replied, 'Today you will be with me in Paradise. This is a solemn promise.'"

Let's examine, for a moment, why Jesus told the thief he was saved. What took place at Calvary at that moment that brought a criminal into the Kingdom of heaven?

There are several important points here. Do you remember back in the chapter "A Few Definitions Might Help," where we looked at "fear of the Lord"? Under that definition, we saw that fear of the Lord includes "a deep sense of accountability before God." We also saw in Proverbs 14:27 that "the fear of the Lord is a fountain of life, to depart from the snares of death."

In Luke 23:40–41 the criminal spoke of just such a "fear of the Lord," just such an accountability. "*But the other criminal protested. 'Don't you even fear God when you are dying? We deserve to die for our evil deeds.'*"

He then reached out to Jesus—his salvation: "*Jesus, remember me when you come into your kingdom.*" The important word in this Scripture is *your*. The thief acknowledged and believed that Jesus was God . . . and he was saved only minutes before his death. "And Jesus replied, 'Today you will be with me in Paradise. This is a solemn promise.'"

This brings us back to Proverbs 21:2: "Every way of a man is right in his own eyes: but *the Lord pondereth the hearts.*" The thief is a perfect example of this Scripture. The criminal acknowledged his sinful life, and he acknowledged Jesus as God. He believed. His heart attitude was right.

This is *your* God! Isn't he fabulous?

2 Peter 3:9: ". . . for . . . he is not willing that any should perish . . ."

OT   *Lamentations 3:33:* "For he does not enjoy afflicting men and causing sorrow."

Father, thank you for sending your Son Jesus Christ to pay for my sins. Thank you for revealing to me through your

Word that you do not see my sins as "more" or "less" or "better" or "worse" than others, because I did. Thank you for lifting from my shoulders the heavy load of guilt that I have carried all my life. May I always be grateful and praising you for this gift. In Jesus' name. Amen.

I Must Accept My Sinful Nature

I'VE SAID already that the subject of sin, which has almost always been distasteful to nonbelievers and new believers, has been far from distasteful for me. I was one of those who felt I was *too* sinful. So learning to understand sin has been a real relief from the heavy burdens of guilt I suffered.

For those who don't believe in sin, it is critically important to understand; otherwise the need for a Savior is never understood.

In studying the entire Bible—Old and New Testament alike—one begins to understand that only Jesus Christ led a sinless life. All of the great men of the Bible accept their sinful natures. Let's examine just a few.

DAVID:

OT **Psalm 39:4:** "Lord, make me to know mine end, and the measure of my days, what it is, that I may know how frail I am" (KJV).

OT **Psalm 51:3:** "For I acknowledge my transgressions, and my sin is ever before me" (KJV).

ISAIAH:

OT **Isaiah 64:6–7:** "We are all infected and impure with sin. When we put on our prized robes of [self-] righteousness we find they are but filthy rags. Like autumn leaves we fade, wither and fall. And our sins, like the wind, sweep us away."

JEREMIAH:

OT *Jeremiah 17:9–10:* "The heart is the most deceitful thing
there is, and desperately wicked. No one can really know
how bad it is! Only the Lord knows! . . ."

PAUL:

Romans 7:15–25: "I don't understand myself at all, for I
really want to do what is right, but I can't. I do what I
don't want to—what I hate. I know perfectly well that
what I am doing is wrong, and my bad conscience proves
that I agree with these laws I am breaking. But I can't
help myself, because I'm no longer doing it. It is sin inside
me that is stronger than I am that makes me do these evil
things.

"I know I am rotten through and through so far as my
old sinful nature is concerned. No matter which way I turn
I can't make myself do right. I want to but I can't. When I
want to do good, I don't; and when I try not to do wrong,
I do it anyway. Now if I am doing what I don't want to, it
is plain where the trouble is: sin still has me in its evil
grasp.

"It seems to be a fact of life that when I want to do what
is right, I inevitably do what is wrong. I love to do God's
will so far as my new nature is concerned, but there is
something else deep within me, in my lower nature, that is
at war with my mind and wins the fight and makes me a
slave to the sin that is still within me. In my mind I want
to be God's willing servant but instead I find myself still
enslaved to sin.

"So you see how it is: my new life tells me to do right,
but the old nature that is still inside me loves to sin. *Oh,
what a terrible predicament I'm in! Who will free me from
my slavery to this deadly lower nature? Thank God! It has
been done by Jesus Christ our Lord. He has set me free.*"

SOLOMON:

OT *Ecclesiastes 7:20:* "And there is not a single man in all the
earth who is always good and never sins."

Not even saved ones (as all of the above men were). The difference is our *new* nature. Yes, now we have two natures.

THE OLD SINFUL NATURE:

Romans 7:18–19: ". . . No matter which way I turn I can't make myself do right. I want to but I can't. When I want to do good, I don't; and when I try not to do wrong, I do it anyway."

THE NEW NATURE:

2 Corinthians 5:17: "When someone becomes a Christian he becomes a brand new person inside. He is not the same anymore. A new life has begun!"

These two natures are at war within us. . . .

Romans 7:22–23: "I love to do God's will so far as my new nature is concerned; but there is something else deep within me, in my lower nature [sin nature], that is at war with my mind and wins the fight and makes me a slave to the sin that is still within me."

The difference now is my new nature. As a believer, I still sin, but I can no longer enjoy it! Not only can I not enjoy sinning—my sins grieve me deeply—and the loss of fellowship with God is more than I can bear. You will soon learn why. God has given me a new heart.

At this point we need to take notice of a not-too-wonderful fact, and that is that there *are* consequences for our disobediences (acts of sin). We already know that the spiritual consequence of sin is loss of fellowship with the Lord, but there are also "earthly" consequences for our sins. If a man kills, he may go to jail. If he speeds, he may get a ticket. If he gets a divorce, his children will suffer. If he overeats (gluttony), he will get fat. If he abuses his body, his health will deteriorate. And so on.

A good analogy is that of dropping a stone into a still pool of water. As it falls into the water, it creates a series of ripples that grows wider and wider. Some stones, because of variance in size, create a broader series of ripples than others.

Such it is with the earthly consequences of acts of sin and disobedience.

These earthly consequences are not from God. We have already seen that God has "good plans" for his children. . . .

OT *Jeremiah 29:11:* "For I know the plans I have for you, says the Lord. *They are plans for good **and not for evil**,* to give you a future and a hope."

If we choose not to follow the "good plans" he has for us —and we all do this—we are "missing out on God's glorious ideal" . . . "we are missing the mark." And that's what "sin" is—falling short of God's glorious ideal.

Romans 3:23: "Yes, all have sinned; all fall short of God's glorious ideal."

When we choose not to live within God's glorious ideal, we are stepping out from under the umbrella of protection provided by him, and we experience the earthly consequences of our disobedience. This is not God's doing, but the results of our own doing, which falls right in line with the real adversary, the source of disobedience and the consequences thereof—the devil himself! But we'll talk more about him later.

God speaks very clearly about obedience to the "laws" of man and obedience to him.

1 Peter 2:16: "You are free from the [Mosaic] law, but *that doesn't mean you are free to do wrong.* Live as those who are free to do only God's will at all times."

Disobeying man's laws is disobedience to the Lord. Christ saved us from eternal damnation, but he did not save us from the "earthly consequences" of our sins, though he can if he chooses to.

Paul sums it up for me:

Romans 12:18: "If it be possible, as much as lieth in you, live peaceably with all men" (KJV).

If I can . . . as much as I am able . . . I am to live at peace with my fellow man.

Understanding that I cannot be perfect, as revealed through God's Word, has helped me to understand grace. God doesn't expect perfection from us, but he has given us new hearts—right desires—that we may live as best we can at peace with him and with our fellow man.

O Father, when I realize what you really did for me by sending your Son Jesus to die for my sins, I could weep for the might and power of that demonstration of love. In all other religions in the world man is reaching for God. With Jesus Christ, you reached down to man! There are not enough words in my limited language to praise you adequately. I know, though, Lord, that you look upon our hearts . . . and mine is overflowing with gratitude and praise to you. In the name of Jesus Christ, I pray. Amen.

I Have a New Heart

As WE HAVE just seen, when we accept Jesus Christ we become new creatures. God accomplishes this by giving us a "new heart" and a "new spirit" . . . and this "new heart and spirit" gives us the "right desires."

OT   *Ezekiel 36:26:* "And I will give you a *new heart*—I will give you *new and right desires*—and put a *new spirit* within you. I will take out your stony hearts of sin and give you new hearts of love."

2 Corinthians 5:17: "When someone becomes a Christian he becomes a brand new person inside. He is not the same anymore. A new life has begun!"

(The security of knowing that I am saved by the same faith as the Jews in the wilderness is the rock of support I needed in my life and is what we are all inherently seeking. I see from the above Scriptures that God has *always* handled our heart "problems" in the same way. This consistency and constancy in God's character is very reassuring to me.)

OT   *Numbers 23:21:* "He hath not beheld iniquity in Jacob, neither hath he seen perverseness in Israel; the Lord his God is with him, and the shout of a king is among them" (KJV).

When you study the wilderness journey, you will be absolutely shocked at the rebelliousness and disobedience of the Jews. Yet we see from the above Scripture that God saw no perverseness in them. That is salvation! Isn't God wonderful?

As I said earlier, you may not feel this change immediately, but God promises that it has begun. It's important to believe this promise from God rather than your own feelings. (I learned a long time ago that I can't always trust my feelings.)

All of this happens to us because of a miracle that takes place at the moment we accept Christ. At that moment, the Holy Spirit makes his home within us. We are truly changed. We are given the right desires. We are given a new heart.

This is what the "born again" experience is all about . . . our new hearts and right desires . . . the new spirit within us.

Dear Lord, thank you for my new heart and my new spirit. Thank you for my new desires. Dear Lord, enable me to glorify you in everything I do. In Christ's name I pray. Amen.

God's Righteousness vs. Self-Righteousness
Christ Makes Me Worthy

I DON'T THINK many people ever realize what a great and mighty demonstration of love God gave us through His Son, Jesus Christ . . . and I'll include a lot of Christians in this statement.

Now that we understand our sinful natures, we can take a deeper look at what God really did for us.

God is holy . . . and righteous . . . pure . . . and perfect. He cannot look upon anything unclean or sinful.

OT *Habakkuk 1:12–13:* "Art thou not from everlasting, O Lord my God, mine Holy One? We shall not die. O Lord, thou hast ordained them for judgment; and, O mighty God, thou hast established them for correction. *Thou art of purer eyes than to behold evil, and canst not look on iniquity:* wherefore lookest thou upon them that deal treacherously, and holdest thy tongue when the wicked devoureth the man that is more righteous than he?" (KJV).

OT *Isaiah 59:1–2:* "Listen now! The Lord isn't too weak to save you. And he isn't getting deaf! He can hear you when you call! But *the trouble is that your sins have cut you off from God. Because of sin he has turned his face away from you and will not listen anymore.*"

OT *Psalm 66:18:* "If I regard iniquity in my heart, the Lord will *not hear me*" (KJV).

But God created us to love . . . and to be loved by us. So . . . what did God do about his disobedient children? What did he do to reconcile this separation?

2 Corinthians 5:21: "For God took the sinless Christ and

poured into him our sins. Then, in exchange, he poured God's goodness into us!"

Colossians 1:20–23: "It was through what his Son did that God cleared a path for everything to come to him—all things in heaven and on earth—for *Christ's death on the cross has made peace with God for all by his blood.* This includes you who were once so far away from God. You were his enemies and hated him and were separated from him by your evil thoughts and actions, yet now he has brought you back as his friends. *He has done this through the death on the cross of his own human body, and now as a result Christ has brought you into the very presence of God, and you are standing there before him with nothing left against you*—nothing left that he could even chide you for; *the only condition is that you fully believe the Truth, standing in it steadfast and firm, strong in the Lord, convinced of the Good News that Jesus died for you, and never shifting from trusting him to save you.* This is the wonderful news that came to each of you and is now spreading all over the world. And I, Paul, have the joy of telling it to others."

1 John 2:2: "*He is the One who took God's wrath against our sins upon himself, and brought us into fellowship with God;* and he is the forgiveness for our sins, and not only ours but all the world's."

OT   *Isaiah 53:4–5:* "*Yet it was our grief he bore, our sorrows that weighed him down.* And we thought his troubles were a punishment from God, for his own sins! But *he was wounded and bruised for our sins. He was chastised that we might have peace; he was lashed—and we were healed!*" [This is a prophecy in the Old Testament of the coming Messiah.]

1 Peter 1:18–19: "God paid a ransom to save you from the impossible road to heaven which your fathers tried to take, and the ransom he paid was not mere gold or silver, as you very well know. But *he paid for you with the precious lifeblood of Christ, the sinless, spotless Lamb of God.*"

Philippians 3:9: "And be found in him, *not having mine own righteousness, which is of the law, but that which is through the faith of Christ, the righteousness which is of God by faith"* (KJV).

1 Corinthians 1:30: "For it is from God alone that you have your life through Christ Jesus. *He showed us God's plan of salvation; he was the one who made us acceptable to God; he made us pure and holy and gave himself to purchase our salvation."*

Romans 5:1: "So now, *since we have been made right in God's sight by faith in his promises, we can have real peace with him because of what Jesus Christ our Lord has done for us."*

Romans 5:6: "When we were utterly helpless with no way of escape, *Christ came at just the right time and died for us sinners* who had no use for him."

Romans 5:8: "But God showed his great love for us by sending Christ to die for us while we were still sinners."

Romans 5:18: "Yes, Adam's sin brought punishment to all, but *Christ's righteousness makes men right with God,* so that they can live."

1 John 4:10: "*In this act we see what real love is: It is not our love for God but his love for us* when he sent his Son to satisfy God's anger against our sins."

Man cannot make himself worthy for salvation by being good enough, by "trying real hard" to do the right thing, by going to church every Sunday nor by trying to keep the Ten Commandments (because no one can). This is "self-righteousness" . . . not God's righteousness.

OT   **Proverbs 14:12:** "There is a way which seemeth right unto a man, but the end thereof are the ways of death" (KJV).

Romans 10:3–4: "For they don't understand that Christ has died to make them right with God. *Instead they are trying to make themselves good enough to gain God's favor by keeping the Jewish laws and customs, but that is not God's way of salvation.* They don't understand that Christ gives to those who trust in him everything they are trying to get by keeping his laws. *He ends all of that."*

Galatians 3:23–26: "Until Christ came we were guarded by the law, kept in protective custody, so to speak, until we could believe in the coming Savior. Let me put it another way. *The Jewish laws were our teacher and guide until Christ came to give us right standing with God through our faith.* But now that Christ has come, we don't need those laws any longer to guard us and lead us to him. For now we are all children of God through faith in Jesus Christ."

Philippians 3:9: "And become one with him, *no longer counting on being saved by being good enough or by obeying God's laws,* but by trusting Christ to save me; for God's way of making us right with himself depends on faith—counting on Christ alone."

1 Timothy 1:8–9: "Those laws are good when used as God intended. *But they were not made for us, whom God has saved;* they are for sinners who hate God, have rebellious hearts, curse and swear, attack their fathers and mothers, and murder. Yes, *these laws are made to identify as sinners all who are immoral and impure:* homosexuals, kidnappers, liars, and all others who do things that contradict the glorious Good News [Jesus] of our blessed God, whose messenger I [Paul] am."

Romans 5:20: "*The Ten Commandments were given so that all could see the extent of their failure to obey God's laws.* But the more we see our sinfulness, the more we see God's abounding grace forgiving us."

Acts 13:39: "Everyone who trusts in him is freed from all guilt and declared righteous—something the Jewish law could never do."

The Bible is full of "ideals" for living, and mankind needs very much to know what those ideals for living are, because it is those ideals that "stretch us." At the same time, it is those ideals that manifest an awareness within us of our "humanness" . . . because there is no way we can live them.

The ideals were in no way meant to cause us to be "uptight" about ourselves or about others. That is not grace. The Greek word for grace, *charis,* translates as "the *divine* influence upon the heart, and its reflection in the life; including: acceptable, benefit, favour, gift, grace, joy, liberality, pleasure, and thanks." It doesn't say a word about "uptight."

This is still further evidence that grace begins "in the heart."

OT   *Ezekiel 36:26:* "And I will give you a new heart—I will give
you new and right desires—and put a new spirit with
you. . . ."

Grace is not what *we* do, grace is what God does; and I
think the greatest example of grace is the Bible itself. God
wrote the Bible (with all of its ideals) through and about
men who could not and never did live them! It's true that
they grew and were stretched everyday—as we will be—
but they were not uptight men and women. This is what
Jesus meant when he said to those who believed:

John 8:31–32: ". . . If ye continue in my Word, then are ye
my disciples indeed; and ye shall know the truth, and the
truth shall make you free" (KJV).

His only condition—continue in my Word . . . stay close
to me . . . and I will set you free.

John 8:36: "If the Son therefore shall make you free, ye
shall be free indeed" (KJV).

Grace "stretches" us. Self-righteousness makes us "up-tight."
Jesus left us with only two commandments.

Matthew 22:37–40: "Jesus replied; "Love the Lord your God
with all your heart, soul and mind." This is the first and
greatest commandment. The second most important is
similar:" Love your neighbor as much as you love yourself." *All the other commandments and all the demands of
the prophets stem from these two laws and are fulfilled if
you obey them.* Keep only these and you will find that you
are obeying all the others.' "

Remember? It always comes back to our heart attitudes.

OT   *Proverbs 21:2:* "Every way of a man is right in his own eyes:
but *the Lord pondereth the hearts*" (KJV).

God understands us so much better than we understand ourselves. He is the Creator! Should he *not* understand his
creatures? He loves us with a love we can only vaguely understand and *never really understand* (until we get to
heaven).

OT   *Ezekiel 11:19–20:* "I will give you one heart and a new
Spirit; I will take from you your hearts of stone and give
you tender hearts of love for God, so that you can obey
my laws and be my people, and I will be your God."

Matthew 11:28–30: "Come unto me, all ye that labour and

are heavy laden, and I will give you rest. Take my yoke upon you, and learn of me; for I am meek and lowly in heart; and ye shall find rest unto your souls. For my yoke is easy, and my burden is light" (KJV).

My Lord, how can I praise you enough? How can I thank you enough? My human heart cannot fathom your unconditional love for me. All I know is that I love it that you love me this much. It is a balm to my wounds of this life . . . a heavenly nectar to my previously unquenchable thirst. I praise you in the name of your Son, Jesus Christ. Amen.

As a Christian, What Do I Do with My Sins?

WHEN WE ACCEPT Jesus Christ as Lord and Savior, we are reconciled with God and are given eternal life with him . . . and yet we still have a sinful nature, which causes us to commit acts of sin all the time. These acts of sin cause a break in our fellowship with God, but this does not mean we lose our salvation. That has been promised and God cannot lie! What I *do* lose temporarily is my fellowship (communication) with him.

OT *Isaiah 59:1–2:* "Listen now! The Lord isn't too weak to save you. And he isn't getting deaf! He can hear you when you call! But the trouble is that *your sins have cut you off from God. Because of sin he has turned his face away from you and will not listen anymore.*"

OT *Psalm 66:18:* "*If I regard iniquity in my heart, the Lord will not hear me*" (KJV).

So what do I do about my sins? How do I regain my fellowship with him?

In order to stay in fellowship with God, I must confess my sins to him and ask to be cleansed and forgiven. Confession does not mean broadly saying, "I have sinned." God expects us to be specific about what our sins are. Otherwise, we would have no awareness really of what sins are in our own particular lives and they are then too easy to overlook or commit again.

1 John 1:9: "But if we confess our sins to him, he can be depended on to forgive us and to cleanse us from every wrong. [And it is perfectly proper for God to do this for us because Christ died to wash away our sins.]" (Brackets not mine.)

OT *Proverbs 28:13:* "A man who refuses to admit his mistakes can never be successful. But if he confesses and forsakes them, he gets another chance."

OT *Psalm 32:5:* "Until I finally stopped trying to hide them. I admitted all my sins to you and said to myself, 'I will confess them to the Lord.' And you forgave me! All my guilt is gone."

OT *Psalm 130:1–8:* "O Lord, from the depths of despair I cry for your help: 'Hear me! Answer! Help me!' Lord, if you keep in mind our sins then who can ever get an answer to his prayers? But you forgive! What an awesome thing this is! That is why I wait expectantly, trusting God to help, for he has promised. I long for him more than sentinels long for the dawn. O Israel, hope in the Lord; for he is loving and kind, and comes to us with armloads of salvation. *He himself shall ransom Israel from her slavery to sin.*"

Forgiveness requires true and sincere repentance, and, once again, repentance is a "heart attitude." If I am not quite ready to repent, then the next best thing is honesty. For instance, if someone has been ugly to me and I am not yet ready to forgive that person, I can confess that to God and ask the Holy Spirit to enable me to truly forgive and repent of my resentment and anger. One thing that has helped me with lingering resentments and bitternesses toward others is to send them love in Jesus Christ through prayer. Ask the Lord to bathe that person (or those persons) in the love of Jesus. You cannot believe how much that will free you from ugly thoughts. Try it—you'll like it! And so will the Lord. As long as he sees that I sincerely *want* to forgive and repent (that I have the right heart attitude about it), I believe that I am back in fellowship with him. But, if my anger and resentment start to seethe and boil up again, I'm back out of fellowship with him (because of my heart attitude)! Remember—he knows your heart. Take it to him again and confess it. He understands. . . .

OT *Proverbs 21:2:* "Every way of a man is right in his own eyes: *but the Lord pondereth the hearts.*"

There are no secrets from him . . . I cannot hide my anger from him.

OT *Psalm 44:21:* "Would God not know it? Yes, he knows the secrets of every heart."

. . . But also remember that he is just and merciful and wants fellowship with you as much as you do with him. (That's why he created you!) He will enable you to forgive deep hurts; he will enable you to humble yourself enough to ask for forgiveness when you have hurt someone else. He enables us to rise above our own pettiness. And this is a progressive thing. It doesn't all happen at once. The more I surrender my sins and faults to him, the more he can do with them.

Confession is a vital part of the Christian walk. When I first accepted Christ, I sat down and confessed (to the Lord in private) every sin I could remember ever committing. After I completed that catharsis, I asked the Holy Spirit to bring to my remembrance the ones I could not remember.

OT *Psalm 139:23–24:* "Search me, O God, and know my heart; test my thoughts. Point out anything you find in me that makes you sad, and lead me along the path of everlasting life."

I believe God does not hold us responsible for those sins we do not remember, but I also believe that he delights in answering a prayer in which I ask to be reminded so that I can be cleansed. He is still revealing old sins to me (and probably will be until I leave this old world)! And he is still cleansing me!

OT *Psalm 19:12:* "But how can I ever know what sins are lurking in my heart? Cleanse me from these hidden faults [those I cannot remember and don't even know about]."

OT *Psalm 51:7:* Purge me with hyssop, and I shall be clean; wash me and I shall be whiter than snow" (KJV).

OT *Psalm 51:10:* "Create in me a clean heart, O God, and renew a right spirit within me."

If you are a believer who, years ago, asked Jesus Christ into your life, and you have never known the true fellowship of the Lord . . . if you have never walked in the Spirit . . . try the catharsis of confession. Dedicate a day to ridding yourself of your past sins . . . and then never look back! You will almost certainly see immediate results! The fellowship of the Lord feels so good that you will not want to be out of fellowship for long. And you will know the minute you are!

God promises us over and over in Scripture that if we confess our sins he is faithful to forgive us and cleanse us of all unrighteousness. In fact, he promises that he will even forget our sins.

OT *Jeremiah 31:34:* ". . . for I will forgive their iniquity, and *I will remember their sin no more*" (KJV).

OT *Psalm 103:12:* "As far as the east is from the west, so far hath he removed our transgressions from us" (KJV).

(The east and the west never meet. They run in opposite directions into infinity.)

OT *Isaiah 44:22:* "*I have blotted out like a thick cloud, thy transgressions, and like a cloud, thy sins;* return unto me; for I have redeemed thee" (KJV).

Hebrews 10:17: "And then he adds, '*I will never again remember their sins and lawless deeds.*'"

OT *Isaiah 43:25:* "I, even I, am he who blotteth out thy transgressions *for mine own sake,* and will not remember thy sins" (KJV).

Note here that he blots out our sins for *his* sake. He really loves us that much! He loves our fellowship! Look above at the Scripture Isaiah 44:22. In it he says, "Return unto me." He wants us as much as we want him.

At this point, we need to look at the difference between true guilt and false guilt. If you have confessed your sins, God promises that you are forgiven and cleansed from true guilt. God also promises that he no longer remembers those sins. If after confession and repentance you are still feeling guilty or still feeling the need to confess over and over again the same sin, that is false guilt! Guess who is accusing you of being guilty!

Revelation 12:10: ". . . for the accuser of our brethren [Satan] is cast down, *who accused them before our God day and night*" (KJV).

There is a vast difference between conviction and condemnation. God convicts and Satan condemns!

If this is happening to you, do what Christ did when Satan tempted him in the wilderness.

Matthew 4:10: "Begone, Satan, for . . ."

. . . it is written in 1 John 1:9 that if we confess our sins to God he can be depended upon to forgive and cleanse every wrong.

. . . it is written in Hebrews 10:17 that God will never again remember my sins and lawless deeds.

. . . it is written in Romans 8:1 that there is now no condemnation for those in Christ Jesus.

Don't let Satan get away with keeping you out of fellowship with God and thus keeping you from enjoying the abundant life.

How's it going, babes? Just as physical babies learn to sit up . . . then to crawl . . . then to walk . . . then to run . . . so are we spiritual babes in Christ growing in the same way. It's really a matter of God's timing . . . not ours.

Heavenly Father, give us the patience to grow at your pace. Teach us to rest in you and let you move us along. And, Father, thank you that you forgive our sins as soon as we confess them. Thank you too that you cleanse us of all unrighteousness. Teach us, O Lord, to be sensitive to the Holy Spirit when he reminds us of unconfessed sin. Thank you that you are so fair and just and merciful to your sheep. In Christ's name we pray. Amen.

In Order to Be Forgiven We Must Forgive

JUST AS GOD forgives us for our sins . . . so does he desire the same charitableness toward others from us. Thus, unforgiveness is another form of disobedience and a manifestation of a rebellious heart. How can we ask forgiveness from God for our sins against him and not extend that same generosity to those whose sins hurt us?

Matthew 6:14–15: "Your heavenly Father will forgive you if you forgive those who sin against you; but *if you refuse to forgive them, he will not forgive you.*"

Mark 11:25: "But when you are praying, *first forgive anyone you are holding a grudge against, so that your Father in heaven will forgive you your sins too.*"

Ephesians 4:32: "Instead, be kind to each other, tenderhearted, *forgiving one another, just as God has forgiven you because you belong to Christ.*"

Matthew 18:21–35: "Then Peter came to Him [Jesus] and asked, 'Sir, how often should I forgive a brother who sins against me? Seven times?' 'No!' Jesus replied, 'seventy times seven! The Kingdom of Heaven can be compared to a king who decided to bring his accounts up to date. In the process, one of his debtors was brought in who owed him $10,000,000! He couldn't pay, so the king ordered him sold for the debt, also his wife and children and everything he had. But the man fell down before the king, his face in the dust, and said, "Oh, sir, be patient with me and I will pay it all." Then the king was filled with pity for him and released him and forgave his debt. But when the man left the king, he went to a man who owed him $2,000 and grabbed him by the throat and demanded instant payment. The man fell down before him and begged him to give him a little time. "Be patient and I will pay it," he pled. But his creditor wouldn't wait. He had the man arrested and jailed until the debt would be paid in full. Then the man's friends went to the king and told him what had happened. And the king called before him the man he had forgiven and said, "You evil-hearted wretch! Here I forgave you all that tremendous debt, just because you asked me to—shouldn't you have mercy on others, just as I had mercy on you?" Then the angry king sent the man to the torture chamber until he had paid every last penny due. So shall my heavenly Father do to you if you refuse to truly forgive your brothers.' "

As I wrote earlier, sometimes forgiving others is beyond our human capabilities. But I remind you that the Holy Spirit can fill you so full of his love that it will just overflow to those who have hurt you. This does not come all at once . . . but time and maturity in Christ will bring this blessing into your heart. In the meantime, ask him to enable you, as much as you are able, to forgive. It is your willingness to pray this kind of prayer—the surrender—which God sees. It is your heart attitude.

Did you know that forgiveness includes forgiving yourself? If you refuse to forgive yourself, you are really refusing God's forgiveness, denying that he has forgiven you. Once again, the Holy Spirit will enable you to do this. Ask him to do this for you.

Why? Not only because it is a sin *not* to forgive yourself but because you must love yourself before you can really love anyone else.

Matthew 22:39: ". . . Thou shalt love thy neighbor *as thyself*" (KJV).

Self-love and self-centeredness are not the same thing. The Christian love story is the greatest love story ever told, but, in order to enjoy it in all its splendor, you must learn to love yourself. But how do you do that?

Knowing that God loves me the way he does has really done a lot for my self-image (which was very bad). Did you know that God knew you before you were in your mother's womb? He loved you and wanted you (that's why he created you), before you were in your mother's womb! Isn't that incredible! My real reason for being on this earth is because *God* wanted me here!

OT   *Jeremiah 1:4–5:* "The Lord said to me, 'I knew you before you were formed within your mother's womb . . .'"

OT   *Psalm 139:13–16:* "You made all the delicate, inner parts of my body, and knit them together in my mother's womb. Thank you for making me so wonderfully complex. It is amazing to think about. Your workmanship is marvelous—and how well I know it. You were there while I was being formed in utter seclusion. You saw me before I was born and scheduled each day of my life before I began to breathe. Every day was recorded in your Book!"

Bask in his love! Praise him for his love! Enjoy the freedom he offers you through love and obedience to him!

O Lord, your love is so bountiful! You fill my heart to overflowing! How wonderful of you to give us your Word—to speak through the written Word to your lost little children. Help them to love themselves. We praise your holy name. In Christ's name. Amen.

The Love Story Continues

THE CHRISTIAN STORY is a love story . . . and our relationship with Jesus Christ is a real love affair. God loves us so much that he has really done it all. This is not to say that the Christian life is one of ease, because it isn't. It has never been easy for the flesh to yield to the spirit. Yielding is preceded by trust and mankind is not only skeptical but prideful. Mankind has always thought he could do it better than the Lord. All he has ever asked of us is to surrender—to relax. To use a familiar expression: Let go and let God; trust. God does not require anything of us that he will not first enable us to do. Even trusting! If I ask him sincerely to enable me to trust him, he will do it.

Trusting in him brings many rewards. The Bible is overflowing with Scripture about those rewards.

Philippians 1:6: "And I am sure that God who began the good work within you will keep right on helping you grow in his grace until his task within you is finally finished on that day when Jesus Christ returns."

Hebrews 4:9: "There remaineth therefore a rest to the people of God" (KJV). [Let go and let God!]

OT *Isaiah 58:11:* "And the Lord shall guide thee continually, and satisfy thy soul in drought, and make fat thy bones; and thou shalt be like a watered garden, and like a spring of water, whose waters fail not" (KJV).

OT *Isaiah 30:21:* "And thine ears shall hear a word behind thee, saying, This is the way, walk ye in it, when ye turn to the right hand, and when ye turn to the left" (KJV).

OT *Isaiah 40:31:* "But *they that wait upon the Lord shall renew their strength.* They shall mount up with wings like eagles; they shall run and not be weary; they shall walk and not faint."

Ephesians 3:16: "That out of his glorious, unlimited resources *he will give you the mighty inner strengthening of his Holy Spirit.*"

Philippians 4:13: "For I can do everything God asks me *with the help of Christ who gives me the strength and power.*"

OT **2 Samuel 22:33:** "God is my strong fortress; *he has made me safe.*"

OT **Psalm 32:8:** "*I will instruct you (says the Lord) and guide you along the best pathway for your life; I will advise you and watch your progress.*"

OT **Psalm 56:13:** "*For you have saved me from death and kept my feet from slipping,* so that I can walk before the Lord in the land of the living."

OT **Psalm 138:8:** "The Lord will work out his plans for my life. . . ."

OT **Ezekiel 11:19–20:** "*I will give you one heart and a new spirit;* I will take from you your hearts of stone *and give you tender hearts of love for God, so that you can obey my laws and be my people, and I will be your God.*"

Romans 10:4: "They don't understand that *Christ gives to those who trust in him everything they are trying to get by keeping his laws. He ends all of that.*"

OT **Isaiah 30:18:** "Yet the Lord still waits for you to come to him, so he can show you his love; he will conquer you to bless you, just as he said. For *the Lord is faithful to his promises. Blessed are all those who wait for him to help them.*"

One of the reasons people are reluctant to commit their lives to Christ is they think they are going to have to "straighten up." They somehow believe that being a Christian is too difficult, when in fact it is the easiest way. "It is a rest to the people of God."

Jude 24: "And now—all glory to him who alone is God, who saves us through Jesus Christ our Lord; yes, splendor and majesty, all power and authority are his from the beginning; his they are and his they evermore shall be. And *he is able to keep you from slipping and falling away, and to* *bring you, sinless and perfect, into his glorious presence with mighty shouts of everlasting joy.* Amen."

2 Peter 1:2–3: "Do you want more and more of God's kindness and peace? Then learn to know him better and better. For *as you know him better, he will give you, through his great power, everything you need for living a truly good life:* He even shares his own glory and his own goodness with us!"

Rest in him.

OT *Psalm 37:7:* "*Rest in the Lord,* and wait patiently for him . . . " (KJV).

OT *Exodus 33:14:* "And he said, My presence shall go with thee, and *I will give thee rest*" (KJV).

Matthew 11:28: "Come unto me, all ye that labor and are heavy laden, and *I will give you rest*" (KJV).

My "spiritual mother" and very close friend, Janis Coffee, says in her testimony that the Lord isn't changing her into some stranger she doesn't recognize; but rather, he is enabling her to be what she has always wanted to be—and more! He enables his children, through the power of his Holy Spirit, to grow toward their maximum potential. Only he knows what the human potential really is.

As you grow confident of his presence, you will also grow to understand that we didn't just "happen." God would never just let things happen "as they may." Everything in the universe is on a perfect timetable.

OT *Psalm 19:1–3:* "The heavens are telling the glory of God; they are a marvelous display of his craftsmanship. Day and night they keep on telling about God. Without a sound or word, silent in the skies, their message reaches out to all the world. . . ."

The problem with mankind is that we have too small a view of God! We picture him with our human minds and see him as like us. But he isn't. He is God.

OT *Isaiah 55:8–9:* "For my thoughts are not your thoughts, neither are your ways my ways, saith the Lord. For as the heavens are higher than the earth, so are my ways higher than your ways, and my thoughts than your thoughts" (KJV).

In an overall study of the Bible, you will see how detail-conscious he is. You will see the deeply personal interest he takes in his children. He will, because he is the Creator, enable you, his creation, to be all you ever dreamed, and more . . . if you will do it his way . . . if you will "walk in the Spirit." It's a real adventure to see what each new day will bring!

Okay . . . this is your last admonition to move slowly through the Word and let the Holy Spirit teach you. You are mature enough by now to depend upon the Holy Spirit to move you at his pace. Keep your spiritual ears open for his leading.

Thank you, dear Lord, for your unfathomable and unending love for your children. How it has changed my life! O Lord, change the life of your child who is studying and learning about you in this book. Teach this child to trust in you . . . to rest in you. Teach this child of yours what it means to "walk in the Spirit." For it is in your precious Son's name that we pray. Amen.

Communication Is Essential to Every Relationship

PRAYER IS communication between you and God that goes not one way but two. Quality prayer is an essential part of "walking in the Spirit," just as quality communication is essential to every relationship. It is a special time between you and him. Without it, there is no communication!

It's so important as a new believer to make a certain amount of time each day for this communication. It's best too if it's the same time and same place every day. This builds a good prayer habit. After awhile, it develops from a "prayer time" or "habit" into a line of communication that is open and going almost continuously. It becomes spontaneous and free and flowing. Prayer will become, in time, as much a part of your "heart attitude" as your desire to love and obey him. In fact, it is all so integrally interwoven that it can't be separated.

Matthew 26:41: "Keep alert and pray. Otherwise temptation will overpower you. For the spirit indeed is willing, but how weak the body is!"

Ephesians 6:18: "Pray all the time. Ask God for anything in line with the Holy Spirit's wishes. Plead with him, reminding him of your needs, and keep praying earnestly for all Christians everywhere."

I talk to the Lord as if I were talking to my best friend. As a matter of fact, I *am* talking to my best friend. My prayers, as you have probably already noticed, are not formal, poetic, nor particularly beautifully expressed. Once again, it is the heart attitude upon which God looks.

Matthew 6:6–8: "But when you pray, go away by yourself,

all alone, and shut the door behind you and pray to your
Father secretly, and your Father, who knows your secrets,
will reward you. Don't recite the same prayer over and
over as the heathen do, who think prayers are answered
only by repeating them again and again. Remember, your
Father knows exactly what you need even before you ask
him!"

Did you notice the last sentence of the last Scripture? *"Your
Father knows exactly what you need even before you ask
him!"* Not only does he know before you ask . . . sometimes
he even *answers* before you ask!

OT   *Isaiah 65:24:* "*I will answer them before they even call to
me.* While they are still talking to me about their needs, I
will go ahead and answer their prayers!"

I have heard many people say they only pray about crises,
that they don't want to "bother" the Lord with the little
problems. This makes me giggle! (It also makes me sad for
those who have such a small view of God.) I giggle because
this attitude reminds me of the tourist who loves to visit a
place but "wouldn't want to live there."

If God knew us before we were in our mother's womb
. . . if he truly created us to love and be loved by him . . .
if he is the God who tended diligently to every detail in
nature . . . then he *must* be interested in every detail
about us!

He tells us to pray constantly.

1 Thessalonians 5:17: "Pray without ceasing" (KJV).
This could not possibly mean that I am only to pray about
crises! We are more significant to God than we realize! We
are so significant that he created us in his image! Try to
understand how much he loves you.

Praying without ceasing builds the line of communication
between you and the Lord which will enable you to hear
his answers when you need them. Praying about the "little
things" will teach you to be sensitive, to hear with your
"inner ear"—your "spiritual ears"—in times of real crises.

Prayer is not only a way of making our needs known to
God. Prayer is a way of showing God how much we love
him, of giving him the praise he so richly deserves . . . not
only because he deserves it, but because it pours forth from

our hearts in love and gratitude for his mercy and love and justice toward us.

WORSHIP HIM FOR WHO HE IS:

OT   *Psalm 100:4:* "Go through his open gates with great thanksgiving; enter his courts with praise. Give thanks to him and bless his name."

OT   *Psalm 42:4:* "When I remember these things, I pour out my soul in me: for I had gone with the multitude, I went with them to the house of God, with the voice of joy and praise, with a multitude that kept holyday" (KJV).

OT   *Psalm 47:1,6,7:* "O clap your hands, all ye people, shout unto God with the voice of triumph. Sing praises to God, sing praises: sing praises unto our King, sing praises. For God is the King of all the earth: sing ye praises with understanding" (KJV).

OT   *Psalm 63:3–6:* "Because thy lovingkindness is better than life, my lips shall praise thee. Thus will I bless thee while I live: I will lift up my hands in thy name. My soul shall be satisfied as with marrow and fatness; and my mouth shall praise thee with joyful lips: When I remember thee upon my bed, and meditate on thee in the night watches" (KJV).

OT   *Isaiah 25:1:* "O Lord, thou art my God; I will exalt thee, I will praise thy name; for thou hast done wonderful things; thy counsels of old are faithfulness and truth."

We praise God with our lips through our prayers. We praise him from the depths of our hearts. But the greatest form of praise is through our lives, our walk with him . . . the "garment of praise" (KJV).

OT   *Isaiah 61:1,3:* "The spirit of the Lord is upon me, because the Lord has anointed me to . . . give . . . *the garment of praise* . . ." (KJV).

CONFESS YOUR SINS:

Before coming to the Lord with your needs for yourself and for others, confess your sins to him, and ask him to reveal the sins you have forgotten or are unaware of.

OT   *Psalm 139:23–24:* "Search me, O God, and know my heart;

test my thoughts. Point out anything you find in me that makes you sad, and lead me along the path of everlasting life."

1 John 1:9: ". . . if we confess our sins to him, he can be depended on to forgive us and to cleanse us from every wrong."

OT *Isaiah 1:18:* ". . . though your sins be as scarlet, they shall be as white as snow; though they be red like crimson, they shall be as wool" (*Amplified Bible*).

Now you can come before him cleansed and pure, washed in the blood of the Lamb.

OT *Exodus 22:27:* ". . . and it shall come to pass, when he crieth unto me, that I will hear; for I am gracious" (KJV).

Tell Him Your Needs:

Philippians 4:6–7: "Don't worry about anything; instead, *pray about everything;* tell God your needs and don't forget to thank him for his answers. If you do this you will experience God's peace, which is far more wonderful than the human mind can understand. His peace will keep your thoughts and your hearts quiet and at rest as you trust in Christ Jesus."

Colossians 4:2: "*Don't be weary in prayer; keep at it;* watch for God's answers and remember to be thankful when they come."

1 Peter 5:7: "*Let him have all your worries and cares,* for he is always thinking about you and watching everything that concerns you."

Pray for Others and Their Needs:

One of our greatest privileges as Christians is to pray on behalf of others.

1 Timothy 2:1: "Here are my directions: *Pray much for others;* plead for God's mercy upon them; give thanks for all he is doing for them."

Ephesians 6:18: ". . . *keep praying earnestly for all Christians everywhere.*"

James 5:16: "Admit your faults to one another and *pray for each other* so that you may be healed. The earnest prayer of a righteous man has great power and wonderful results."

PRAY FOR GOD'S PERFECT WILL:

God's will and desire for our lives may not coincide with what our personal wills and desires are for ourselves. But we already know that God holds the master plan. He knows and wants what is best for us.

OT *Psalm 139:16: "You saw me before I was born and scheduled each day of my life before I began to breathe. Every day was recorded in your Book!"*

OT *Jeremiah 29:11: "For I know the plans I have for you, says the Lord. They are plans for good and not for evil, to give you a future and a hope."*

Thus, when we pray for God's will in our lives, we know that we can trust him because he has our best interest at heart.

How *do* you pray for God's perfect will? Well, the Holy Spirit will enable you to do that.

Romans 8:26–27: "And in the same way—by our faith—the Holy Spirit helps us with our daily problems and in our praying. For we don't even know what we should pray for, nor how to pray as we should; but the Holy Spirit prays for us with such feeling that it cannot be expressed in words."

Jesus left us an example for facing every situation man is faced with in life. One of the most beautiful ones was the one of surrender of his will to his Father. Before he was crucified, in a deeply touching moment between him and his father, he cried out in anguish to be spared the horrible ordeal of agonizing death on the cross.

Matthew 26:39: "He went forward a little, and fell face downward on the ground, and prayed, 'My Father! If it is possible, let this cup [crucifixion] be taken away from me. But I want your will, not mine.'"

. . . And to be spared the ordeal of actually becoming sin for us (2 Cor. 5:21, "For God took the sinless Christ and poured into him our sins") and thereby being separated (even briefly) from his beloved Father—in whom and with whom he had abided throughout eternity—because God cannot look upon sin (Hab. 1:13). (Remember his anguished cry? ". . . My God, my God, why hast thou forsaken me?" [Mark 15:34, KJV]) Jesus, who *was* God, our Creator, for that brief moment in time, was separated from the Godhead, the Father and Holy Spirit. And *yet he yielded to God's perfect will.* What if he hadn't? What would have happened to God's creatures?

But he did . . .

Hebrews 5:7–9: "Yet while Christ was here on earth he pleaded with God, praying with tears and agony of soul to the only one who would save Him from [premature] death. And God heard his prayers because of his strong desire to obey God at all times. And even though Jesus was God's Son, he had to learn from experience what it was like to obey, when obeying meant suffering. It was after he had proved himself perfect in this experience that Jesus became the Giver of eternal salvation to all those who obey him" (brackets not mine).

. . . And . . .

2 Corinthians 5:21: ". . . Then, in exchange, he poured God's goodness into us!"

Pray for God's perfect will in your life.

1 John 5:14: "And this is the confidence that we have in him, that, if we ask anything according to his will, he heareth us" (KJV).

PRAY IN JESUS' NAME:

John 14:13–14: "You can ask him for anything, *using my name,* and I will do it, for this will bring praise to the Father because of what I, the Son, will do for you. Yes, ask anything, *using my name,* and I will do it!"

John 16:26: "At that day ye shall *ask in my name,* and I say not unto you, that I will pray the Father for you" (KJV).

PRAISE HIM FOR ANSWERED PRAYER:

Keep your "spiritual eyes and ears" open to God's answers to your prayers and give him thanks for the love he pours out on you everyday.

OT **Psalm 50:14:** "What I want from you is your true thanks . . ."

OT **Psalm 30:4:** "Oh, sing to him you saints of his; *give thanks to his holy name.*"

Colossians 4:2: "Don't be weary in prayer; keep at it; *watch for God's answers and remember to be thankful when they come.*"

OT **Psalm 138:1–4:** "Lord, with all my heart I thank you. I will sing your praises before the armies of angels in heaven. I face your Temple as I worship, giving thanks to you for all your lovingkindness and your faithfulness, for your promises are backed by all honor of your name. When I pray, you answer me, and encourage me by giving me the strength I need. Every king in all the earth shall give you thanks, O Lord, for all of them shall hear your voice."

As you are learning from studying God's Word, his most powerful means of communication with his children is through his Word. As you continue to study, you will see that the Bible is a very mystical book with many levels of understanding. There is no way man can learn it all or know it all. Yet the Bible is so simple and clear that even a "babe" can learn about God's love and plans for his children.

God's Word is God's will for his children! If you know the Scripture, you know God's will and you know what his promises for you are. If you know what the promises are, then you can "claim" ("stand on") his promises and pray the Word back to God. This is music to his ears, because you are praying for God's perfect will when you do this. Praying the promises of the Word back to God is not difficult. Here are just a few examples. Try it . . .

Heavenly Father, thank you for your beautiful Word. Thank you for the many wonderful promises in the Bible. Thank you that . . .

. . . it is written in Ezekiel 36:26 that you will give me a new heart—you will give me new and right desires —and put a new spirit within me. I claim this promise in Jesus' name.

. . . it is written in 1 John 1:9 that if I confess my sins to you, you can be depended on to forgive me and to cleanse me from every wrong. I claim this promise in Jesus' name.

. . . it is written in Hebrews 13:5 that you will never leave me nor forsake me. I claim this promise in Jesus' name.

. . . it is written in Isaiah 49:16 that you have engraved me in the palm of your hand. I claim this promise in Jesus' name.

. . . it is written in John 10:29 that no man can pluck me from your hand. I claim this promise in Jesus' name.

. . . it is written in Hebrews 13:8 that you never change—that you are the same yesterday, today, and forever. I claim this promise in Jesus' name.

. . . it is written in Isaiah 54:13 that my children shall be taught of the Lord and great will be the peace of my children. I claim this promise in Jesus' name.

. . . it is written in Isaiah 55:11 that your Word is sent out by you and always produces fruit—that it will accomplish all that you want it to and it will prosper everywhere you send it. I claim this promise in Jesus' name.

. . . it is written in Psalm 147:18 that you will send forth your Word and it will melt me. I claim this promise in Jesus' name.

. . . it is written in John 14:6 that Jesus is the Way, the Truth and the Life, and that I can come to you through him. I claim this promise in Jesus' name.

. . . it is written in John 8:31–32 that if I continue in your Word I will know the Truth and the Truth will set me free. I claim this promise in Jesus' name.

. . . it is written in 1 Corinthians 1:20 that Christ carries out and fulfills all of your promises, no matter how many of them there are. I claim this promise in Jesus' name.

. . . it is written in Galatians 3:29 that I am now Christ's and am a true descendant of Abraham, and, therefore, that all of your promises to him belong to me. I claim this promise in Jesus' name.

. . . it is written in 1 Kings 8:56 that not one word has failed of all the wonderful promises proclaimed by your servant Moses. I claim this promise in Jesus' name.

. . . it is written in Romans 4:21 that I can be sure that you are well able to do anything you promise. I claim this promise in Jesus' name.

There are hundreds and hundreds of promises in God's Word (7700, to be exact). I have given you only a few illustrations . . . but doesn't this excite you? The wealth that is in the Bible is unlimited. Avail yourself of God's riches!

And finally . . .

Philippians 4:8–9: "And now, brothers, as I close this letter let me say this one more thing: Fix your thoughts on what is true and good and right. Think about things that are pure and lovely, and dwell on the fine, good things in others. Think about all you can praise God for and be glad about."

OT   *Deuteronomy 6:4–9:* "O Israel, listen: Jehovah is our God, Jehovah alone. You must love him with all your heart, soul, and might. And you must think constantly about these commandments I am giving you today. You must teach them to your children and talk about them when you are at home or out for a walk; at bedtime and the first thing in the morning. Tie them on your finger, wear them on your forehead, and write them on the doorposts of your house!"

John 14:27: "Peace I leave with you, my peace I give unto you: not as the world giveth, give I unto you. *Let not your heart be troubled, neither let it be afraid*" (KJV).

Dear, sweet Lord, thank you that you hear my prayers . . . thank you that I don't have to pray "perfectly." Enable me, Lord, to let the Spirit pray through me that I may pray for your perfect will. Thank you, dear Lord, that you love me and want the very best for me. Help me to understand this when what I think is best and what you think is best aren't the same. Help me to see that you, and only you, work all things together for good for those who love you. In Jesus' name I pray. Amen.

The Body of Christ—God's Family

THE BODY OF Christ is another one of those "bonuses" God gives to his children. The Body of Christ is the Church—not the buildings . . . but the people of Jesus Christ.

Ephesians 1:22–23: "And God has put all things under his feet and made him [Jesus] the supreme Head of *the church—which is his body,* filled with himself, the Author and Giver of everything everywhere."

Colossians 1:18: "He is the Head of *the body made up of his people—that is, his church*—which he began. . . ."

The Greek word for church is *ekklesia,* which translates as "called-out ones." These called-out ones are God's family . . . and mine—a family with a common bond and that bond is Jesus Christ.

1 Peter 3:8: "And now this word to all of you: *You should be like one big happy family,* full of sympathy toward each other, loving one another with tender hearts and humble minds."

Ephesians 4:16: "*Under his direction the whole body is fitted together perfectly, and each part in its own special way helps the other parts,* so that the whole body is healthy and growing and full of love."

Romans 12:4–5: "Just as there are many parts to our [human] bodies, so it is with Christ's body. We are all parts of it, and it takes every one of us to make it complete, for we each have different work to do. *So we belong to each other, and each needs all the others.*"

1 Corinthians 10:17: "No matter how many of us there are, *we all eat from the same loaf, showing that we are all parts of the one body of Christ.*"

1 Corinthians 12:12–13: "Our bodies have many parts, but the many parts make up only one body when they are all put together. *So it is with the 'body' of Christ. Each of us is a part of the one body of Christ.* Some of us are Jews, some are Gentiles, some are slaves and some are free. But the Holy Spirit has fitted us all together into one body. *We have been baptized into Christ's body by the one Spirit, and have all been given that same Holy Spirit.*"

We *are* one body . . . and we are to stand together, to learn from one another, encourage our brothers and sisters.

Colossians 2:2: "This is what I have asked of God for you: that you will be encouraged and knit together by strong ties of love, and that you will have the rich experience of knowing Christ with real certainty and clear understanding. . . ."

Hebrews 10:24: "In response to all he has done for us, let us outdo each other in being helpful and kind to each other and in doing good."

1 Thessalonians 5:11: "So encourage each other to build each other up, just as you are already doing."

Because of my painful childhood and young adult life, I had a very poor self-image which left a huge void in my life, an insatiable desire to be loved. Jesus Christ is the only one who could fill that void, but God's family—the body of Christ—has provided me lots of love and support too. There are literally hundreds of people who pray for me regularly. And prayer is a very potent thing. My most special relationships are with other believers who walk in the Spirit. They love me as much as is humanly possible with the unconditional love God calls all of his children to give.

Galatians 6:2: "Bear ye one another's burdens, and so fulfill the law of Christ" (KJV).

OT *Proverbs 17:17:* "A true friend is always loyal, and *a brother is born to help in time of need.*"

I'd like to stop here and return to Romans 12:4 for a moment. "Just as there are many parts to our [human] bodies, so it is with Christ's body. We are all parts of it, and *it takes every one of us to make it complete, for we each have different work to do.* . . ." As I have been writing this chapter, I have been impressed in my spirit, by the Holy Spirit, of a very important part of the Body of Christ in my own life.

I do a lot of public speaking about my relationship with Jesus Christ, and now I am writing this, my first book. To the world this may look very impressive, and very important. Yet, I know in the deepest reaches of my spirit that I could not do any of these things as often nor as well without the prayer support of my brothers and sisters. Almost every time I speak, someone comes up to me and tells me that God has impressed upon them that they are to pray for me on a regular basis. I have had hundreds of people tell me that they are praying for me. This is not spoken in an insincere way, but rather it is clear that these people have a deep desire to pray for me. Intercessory prayer is one of the most important ministries in life, and most Christians participate to some degree, but there are a large number (though never enough) of Christians who spend hours and hours of every day in deep intercession for the troubled, for the sick, for the lost, for our nation, for our nation's leaders, for peace in the world. The needs for intercessory prayer are endless, and it is one of the most important things we can do for the Lord. He will richly bless those who are obedient and willing to give of themselves in this way. Though it may appear on the surface that my job is more important than other jobs, it is increasingly evident to me that I could not do my job without the prayer support of the other members of the Body. "It takes every one of us to make it complete, for we each have different work to do. . . ."

Thank you, Lord, for the wonderful Body of Christ. Thank you brothers and sisters for your support.

Romans 12:9–10: "Don't just pretend that you love others: really love them. Hate what is wrong. Stand on the side of the good. Love each other with brotherly affection and take delight in honoring each other."

1 John 4:16: ". . . God is love, and anyone who lives in love is living with God and God is living in him."

If you don't have Christian friends, pray for God to send some into your life.

Heavenly Father, we pray with thanksgiving for your body of believers . . . for the Body of Christ. Thank you for this beautiful support system, especially for those "behind the scenes." Dear Lord, for them, we pray a special blessing that they might know how very important they are. And, dear Lord, we pray for unity among believers—not necessarily unity in every belief—but unity in your Son Jesus Christ. For it is in his name that we pray. Amen.

You Know You've Really Got It When You Want to Give It Away

WHEN I FIRST became a Christian, the last thing I thought I would ever do was witness for Jesus Christ, tell someone else about him. In fact, there had been several instances in my life where someone had witnessed to me, and I vowed that I would *never* do that! I know now that the negative feelings I had were my own convictions and that the seeds were being planted all along the way.

In any case, I do very often share Jesus Christ when I give my testimony to large groups. But we are also called to share the Gospel, the Good News, on an individual basis as well, because when people come to hear a testimony, they come purposely to hear; yet there are many who never have occasion to hear or have exposure in their lives to the Gospel. So it is up to us, God's ambassadors!

The greatest work we are privileged to do for the Lord is the evangelizing of him. "The degree of your own joy in heaven will be determined by the souls you have had a part in bringing to Christ, just as Paul tells the Thessalonian believers (after he witnessed to them) that they are his 'hope, or joy or crown of rejoicing' now and when Jesus comes again."*

1 *Thessalonians 2:19–20:* "For what is it we live for, that gives us hope and joy and is our proud reward and crown? It is you! Yes, you will bring us much joy as we stand together before our Lord Jesus Christ when he comes back again. For you are our trophy and joy."

2 *Corinthians 2:14:* "But thanks be to God! For through

* *The Christian Life New Testament* (Nashville: Thomas Nelson Inc., 1978), p. 368 n.

what Christ has done, he has triumphed over us so that now wherever we go he uses us to tell others about the Lord and to spread the Gospel like a sweet perfume."
This does not mean that we must go around grabbing lapels and telling people what they should and should not do. This is a very sensitive thing, and you want to wait for the Lord to move you to share the Good News. He will! At first, I "put God on notice" that he would have to arrange for people to ask me first, that I just couldn't *voluntarily* tell. But as I began to share, a wonderful thing began to happen. God revealed to me that he had already prepared the hearts of the ones I shared with and that they were hungry to hear the Good News! Especially now, people know where I stand, and frequently they seek me out to ask me! The world is full of hungry people. Won't you help feed them?
1 Peter 3:15: "Quietly trust yourself to Christ your Lord and if anybody asks why you believe as you do, *be ready to tell him,* and do it *in a gentle and respectful way.*"

OT *Proverbs 11:30:* "Godly men are growing a tree that bears life-giving fruit, and *all who win souls are wise.*"

James 5:20: "That person who brings him [a lost person] back to God will have saved a wandering soul from death, bringing about the forgiveness of his many sins."

Luke 15:10: "In the same way *there is joy in the presence of the angels of God when one sinner repents.*"

OT *Daniel 12:3:* "And those who are wise—the people of God— shall shine as brightly as the sun's brilliance, and *those who turn many to righteousness will glitter like stars forever.*"

The above verses more than reveal the rewards we have as a result of our witnessing. It is an inexpressible joy to watch the seeds you helped plant begin to grow and ultimately bear fruit. I suppose that is all the encouragement I need.

One important thing to remember, especially when you are discouraged by someone who does not respond to your witness (at least not that you can see), is that it is God who does the saving. You are only an agent for him. In fact, Jesus himself told his disciples that some of them would be "sowers of the seed" and some would be "reapers of the crop." In fact, in my own experience, I encountered "sowers," "tillers of the soil," "waterers," and a "reaper." As agents for the Lord, it is not our business to decide on our role, but, rather, to obey his leading—to leave it in his hands —because he is able!

John 4:35–37: "Do you think the work of harvesting will not begin until the summer ends four months from now? Look around you! Vast fields of human souls are ripening all around us, and are ready now for reaping. The reapers will be paid good wages and will be gathering eternal souls into the granaries of heaven! *For it is true that one sows and someone else reaps.*"

2 Corinthians 5:20: "*We are Christ's ambassadors.* God is using us to speak to you: we beg you, as though Christ himself were here pleading with you, receive the love he offers you—be reconciled to God."

Here is where the question "What about those people who never hear about Christ?" comes back into strong focus. Do you remember that God promises that all who seek him in earnest will find him? (Jer. 29:13). We learned that it is not the ones who are earnestly seeking him that we need to worry about, for God promises they will find him. The ones who are *not* seeking him are the ones we should worry about; that is where our witness becomes so important.

Since you are God's ambassador in this mission, the Holy Spirit will be with you to give you the right words to say and the proper timing in which to say them.

1 Corinthians 1:17: "For Christ didn't send me to baptize, but to preach the Gospel; and even my preaching sounds poor, for I do not fill my sermons with profound words and high-sounding ideas, for fear of diluting the mighty power there is in *the simple message of the cross of Christ.*" (Here the Greek word for "preach" translates "to herald [as a public crier], especially divine truth [the gospel].")

Mark 16:15: "And then he told them, 'You are to go into all the world and preach the Good News to everyone, everywhere.'"

The gift of eternal life brings many blessings. Remember the bonuses?

OT   *Isaiah 61:3:* "To all who mourn in Israel he will give:/ Beauty for ashes;/Joy instead of mourning;/Praise in-

stead of heaviness./For God has planted them like strong
and graceful oaks for his own glory."
Wouldn't you love to be a part of sharing these beautiful
gifts with someone? As a matter of fact, there is no greater
gift you could give than an introduction to Jesus Christ,
through whom they can receive eternal life and the
abundant life!!

A word of caution to new believers. Too often we go out
as new Christians and overwhelm everyone we know! *Trust
in the wisdom of the Lord to lead you,* especially where the
spouse is concerned. If your spouse is not yet a believer,
don't swamp him or her with the Good News or it could become bad news between you in a hurry! Jesus does not want
anyone to come to him through force or duress. He wants to
woo us into the great love affair of Christianity. So please
be tender and please be careful. The best witness to all unbelievers, especially to spouses, is the witness of a changed
life. Without a changed life we really have nothing to show
for our faith.

1 Peter 2:12–17: "Be careful how you behave among your
unsaved neighbors; for then, even if they are suspicious
of you and talk against you, they will end up praising
God for your good works when Christ returns. For the
Lord's sake, obey every law of your government: those of
the king as head of the state, and those of the king's of-
ficers, for he has sent them to punish all who do wrong,
and to honor those who do right. It is God's will that your
good lives should silence those who foolishly condemn
the Gospel without knowing what it can do for them,
having never experienced its power. You are free from
the law, but that doesn't mean you are free to do wrong.
Live as those who are free to do only God's will at all
times. Show respect for everyone. Love Christians everywhere. Fear God and honor the government."

2 Corinthians 4:1–2: "It is God himself, in his mercy, who
has given us this wonderful work [of telling his Good
News to others], and so we never give up. We do not try
to trick people into believing—we are not interested in
fooling anyone. We never try to get anyone to believe that
the Bible teaches what it doesn't. All such shameful meth-

ods we forego. We stand in the presence of God as we speak and so we tell the truth, as all who know us will agree." (Brackets not mine.)

2 *Corinthians* 4:6–7: "For God, who said, 'Let there be light in the darkness,' has made us understand that it is the brightness of his glory that is seen in the face of Jesus Christ. But this precious treasure—this light and power that now shine within us—is held in a perishable container, that is, in our weak bodies. Everyone can see that the glorious power within must be from God and is not our own."

Matthew 5:16: "Don't hide your light! Let it shine for all; let your good deeds glow for all to see, so that they will praise your heavenly Father."

OT *Daniel* 12:3: "And those who are wise—the people of God —shall shine as brightly as the sun's brilliance. . . ."

Rely on the Holy Spirit to enable you to share the Good News in a meaningful way.

Acts 1:8: "But when the Holy Spirit has come upon you, *you will receive power to testify about me with great effect. . . .*"

Trust in him and always witness with lots and lots of love.

Dear Lord, enable us to be effective, loving heralds of the Good News of Jesus Christ. Teach us to be sensitive to your guidance and touch. Father, give us the gift of evangelism that those who do not know you may know the Truth. Father, encourage us and help us that our lights may shine. In Jesus' name. Amen.

From Milk to Junior Food to Solid Food

THIS MARKS the end of the "milk" part of the diet (though I did sneak some "solid food" in on you). You are now ready for a bit of solid food.

This last section is devoted to questions either I, as a new believer, had, or questions I have frequently heard from other new believers.

Remember, if it gets to be too much, hang it on a hook! Each time you pick up this book to study, pray diligently that the Holy Spirit will teach you!

Jesus Christ Has Always Been with the Father

WHEN I ACCEPTED Christ, I knew very little about the Bible, or about God. Some way in my mind I thought Jesus was someone (or something) God dreamed up at some point in time to take care of our sins. I was shocked to discover that God the Father, Son and Holy Ghost has *always* existed.

OT *Genesis 1:26:* "And God said, Let *us* make man in *our* image, after *our* likeness . . ." (KJV).

Had you noticed that even in Genesis, God was plural— "us," "our"? Even when Moses wrote Genesis, Jesus was there!

Revelation 1:8: "I [Jesus] am the Alpha and Omega, *the beginning and the ending,* saith the Lord, *which is, and which was, and which is to come,* the Almighty" (KJV).

John 1:1–2: "*Before anything else existed, there was Christ, with God. He has always been alive and is himself God.*"

John 17:5: "And now, Father, reveal my glory as I stand in your presence, *the glory we shared before the world began.*"

Colossians 1:15–16: "*Christ is the exact likeness of the unseen God. He existed before God made anything at all, and, in fact, Christ himself is the Creator who made everything in heaven and earth,* the things we can see and the things we can't; the spirit world with its kings and kingdoms, its rulers and authorities; all were made by Christ for his own use and glory."

John 17:24: "Father, I will that they also, whom thou hast given me, be with me where I am, that they may behold my glory, which thou hast given me; *for thou lovedst me before the foundation of the world*" (KJV).

Please permit me a *non sequitur* here. John 17:24 stirs a response in me that I must share with you. In this verse, Jesus, as he does so many other places in the New Testament, accepts his human nature and surrenders everything to the Father. "Father, I will that they also, *whom thou hast given me*, be with me where I am, that they may behold my glory, *which thou hast given me . . .*" (KJV)—another one of the many beautiful examples of his surrender to the Father that are all through the Gospels.

Philippians 2:5–9: "Your attitude should be the kind that was shown us by Jesus Christ, who, *though he was God, did not demand and cling to his rights as God, but laid aside his mighty power and glory, taking the disguise of a slave and becoming like men.* And he humbled himself even further, going so far as actually to die a criminal's death on a cross. Yet it was because of this that God raised him up to the heights of heaven and gave him a name which is above every name."

That was quite a sacrifice for him. It makes me love him so much! Here he was . . . God! . . . The Alpha and the Omega!

How Can Jesus Be 100 Percent God, Yet 100 Percent Man?

As I SIT HERE and ponder this next section, I find myself overwhelmed with the myriad questions going around in my head. How do I, who do not understand, but emphatically believe, explain to anyone the fact of Jesus, who is completely God and completely man?

Kenneth Boa says in *God, I Don't Understand*, "As long as man sets up his own mind as the standard for truth, he cannot attain a real knowledge of God. The problem of knowing God is solved in one word: revelation. When God's Word, instead of unaided human reasoning, becomes the basis for truth, answers are possible." *

What I hear Mr. Boa saying is that we must study the facts as *God* has revealed them and trust the Holy Spirit to shed the light upon them and reveal the truth.

OT   *Psalm 43:3:* "Oh, send out your light and your truth—let them lead me. . . ."

OT   *Psalm 36:9:* "For you are the Fountain of life; our light is from your Light."

John 16:13: "When the Holy Spirit, who is truth, comes, he shall guide you into all truth, for he will not be presenting his own ideas, but will be passing on to you what he has heard. . . ."

And now, as we pursue God's truth of the God-Man, Jesus, I pray that the Holy Spirit will shed his light on it for you.

JESUS IS PROCLAIMED TO BE GOD:

John 1:1: "In the beginning was the Word, and the Word was with God, and *the Word was God*" (KJV.).

* P. 134.

John 1:14: "And the Word was made flesh, and dwelt among
us (and we beheld his glory, the glory as of the only-
begotten of the Father), full of grace and truth" (KJV).

JESUS HIMSELF PROCLAIMED HIS DEITY:

John 10:30: "*I and my Father are one*" (KJV).
John 14:9: "*. . . He that hath seen me hath seen the Father;*
and how sayest thou then, Show us the Father?" (KJV).
John 8:24: ". . . unless you *believe that I am the Messiah,
the Son of God,* you shall die in your sins."

JESUS WAS ALSO MAN:

John 1:14: "*And the Word was made flesh . . .*" (KJV).

HE HAD A HUMAN BIRTH:

Matthew 1:16: "*. . . Mary, of whom was born Jesus,* who is
called Christ" (KJV).
Luke 2:7: "And *she brought forth her first-born son . . .*"
(KJV).

THE GOD-MAN:

Even though Jesus was 100 percent God, he never exercised
his complete power and authority during his life as a man.
Philippians 2:5-7: ". . . Jesus Christ, who, though he was
God, did not demand and cling to his rights as God, but
laid aside his mighty power and glory, taking the disguise
of a slave and becoming like man."
He was 100 percent man.

The study of the God-Man could go on for a thousand
pages and not come to an end. Since this study is *Milk for
Babes,* we will not pursue this any deeper. My wish for you
is that you will know and understand that Jesus was wholly
God and at the same time wholly man—something our finite
minds can never really grasp.
Colossians 2:9: "*For in Christ there is all of God in a human
body.*"

It's important that you know the facts as God has presented them in order to know what to believe. It's impossible to make an intelligent decision about what you believe without the facts.

Once again quoting Ken Boa, "The real affiliation between the human and the divine in the person of Jesus Christ is an unsolvable mystery, since no one has the intellectual categories which can relate to such a combination." *

Romans 11:34: "For who hath known the mind of the Lord? Or who hath been his counselor?" (KJV).

---

* *God, I Don't Understand*, p. 27.

Why Would God Become a Man?

John 1:1: "In the beginning was the Word, and the Word was with God, and *the Word was God*" (KJV).

John 1:14: "*And the Word was made flesh, and dwelt among us* (and we beheld his glory, the glory as of the only begotten of the Father), full of grace and truth" (KJV).

We have, in the Bible, God's Word. In Jesus Christ, we have the Living Word. One question which seems to baffle the human mind is "Why would God become a man? After all, God is God!"

There is a lovely contemporary parable I have heard many times which really has become part of Christian folklore, and it dearly but profoundly answers this question.

There was once a farmer who totally rejected the idea of the incarnation of God in Jesus Christ—God in the flesh. He refused to attend church or even discuss Jesus Christ with the rest of his family. One Christmas, after they had left him to go to church, he was sitting in his den. It was a cold, blustery day, and there was a little bird which kept hitting the window pane. It was cold and seeking shelter. The farmer, stirred to compassion for the miserable little bird, put on his coat and went outside. He thought, "If I could only get that little bird to go into my barn where it is warm, he wouldn't be in danger of freezing to death or of killing himself by hitting the window pane." So, he opened the barn door and attempted to wave the bird inside. But the little bird was frightened of the farmer and flew away. So the farmer turned the light on inside the barn, thinking, "Perhaps if I turn on the light, the bird will be drawn inside by the light into the warmth and comfort of the barn." But the little bird continued to flutter around frantically in great fear of the farmer. After all, what do birds know about farmers anyway? Then the farmer thought, "I know what I'll do. I'll get a broom and gently guide the bird into the barn." But this frightened the little bird even more. In fact, the little bird's heart was beating so wildly and it was so terrified, that all it could do was fly high into the top of a tree. Oh, how the farmer wanted to extend his love and comfort to that miserable, frightened, freezing little creature. He thought and thought. Finally, the idea came to him, "If only *I* could become a bird. Then I could show it that I don't want to harm it but only want to save it." At that very moment, the farmer fell to his knees and thanked God. He realized that God had just shown him why He became a man—to show his creatures that he doesn't want to hurt us but rather to save us.

What a precious parable. What a mighty God!

1 John 4:19: "We love him, because *he first loved us*" (KJV).

 OT　*Zephaniah 3:17:* "The Lord, thy God, in the midst of thee is mighty; he will save, he will rejoice over thee with joy; he will rest in his love, he will joy over thee with singing" (KJV).

John 3:16: "For God so loved the world, that he gave his only begotten Son, that whosoever believeth in him should not perish, but have everlasting life" (KJV).

How Can the Father, Son, and Holy Spirit Be Three Gods, But One?

THE TRINITY OF God is one of the great mysteries of the Bible. Our human minds cannot begin to comprehend that God is One, yet Three. In order to avoid error about this mystery, remember that with regard to the being of God—he is One; with regard to the personality of God—he is Three.

Before we elaborate on the Trinity, may I share with you a *very* simplistic analogy of the Trinity which was given to me by a wonderful woman, spiritually mature in the Lord for *many years?*

To my children, I am their mother; to my husband, I am his wife; to my mother and father, I am their daughter. I am only one person, yet my roles as mother, wife, and daughter are completely different. I respond differently to my children as their mother than I do to my parents as their daughter, and I respond differently as a wife from the other two roles. But I am one person. This simple analogy cannot "explain" the Trinity of God, because that is unfathomable, yet it has helped many to understand and believe the facts as God has presented them to us.

Scripture says there is but One God!

OT **Deuteronomy 6:4:** "Hear, O Israel! The Lord is our God, *the Lord is one!*" (KJV).

1 Corinthians 8:4: ". . . Well, we all know that an idol is not really a god, and that *there is only one God,* and no other."

OT **Isaiah 45:21–22:** ". . . For *there is no other God but me—* a just *God and a Savior—no, not one!* Let all the world

look to me for salvation! *For I am God; there is no other.*"
Yet Scripture speaks of God as three distinct and separate
"beings" (personalities) . . . even in the Old Testament!

OT   *Isaiah 48:16:* "Come closer and listen. I have always told you
plainly what would happen, so that you could clearly
understand. And now *the Lord God* and *his Spirit* have
sent *me.*" [The "me" speaking here is the Messiah.]

This verse most clearly identifies the Trinity than any other
Old Testament verse.

OT   *Genesis 1:26:* "And God said, Let *us* make man in *our* image,
and after *our* likeness . . ." (KJV).

Notice that God refers to himself here in plural pronouns
. . . God in his Trinity . . . all the way back in chapter
one of book number one—Genesis!

New Testament Scriptures also identify the Trinity.

Matthew 3:16–17: "After his baptism, as soon as Jesus came
up out of the water, the heavens were opened to him and
he saw the *Spirit of God* coming down in the form of a
dove. And *a voice from heaven* [*the Father*] said, 'This is
my beloved Son, and I am wonderfully pleased with
him.'"

Matthew 28:19: "Therefore go and make disciples in all the
nations, baptizing them into the name of the *Father* and
of the *Son* and of the *Holy Spirit.*"

John 14:26: "But when *the Father* sends *the Comforter* instead of me—and *by the Comforter I mean the Holy Spirit*
—he will teach you much, as well as remind you of everything *I myself* [*Jesus*] have told you."

Scripture also attests to the deity of the Father, Son, and
Holy Spirit individually.

John 6:27: ". . . For *God the Father* has sent me for this
very purpose."

Hebrews 1:8: "But *unto the Son he saith, Thy throne, O God,*
is forever and ever . . . (KJV).

Acts 5:3–4: ". . . When you claimed this was the full price,
*you were lying to the Holy Spirit. . . . You weren't lying
to us, but to God.*"

One day I was led to count the number of times the word
God appears in the Old Testament. To take the count quickly
I used *Strong's Exhaustive Concordance,* and possibly I may

be off by a small number. Perfect accuracy is not the important thing here; the point of counting is. The word *God* appears approximately 3,034 times in the Old Testament, and approximately 2,246 of those times the Hebrew word used for *God* is *Elohim*. Now herein lies the point. *Elohim* is the plural form of *El*, which translates "God." Therefore, *Elohim* translates literally "Gods." Seventy-five percent of the time in the Old Testament the word *God* literally translates "Gods"! The other twenty-six percent of the time eight other Hebrew words are used. I thought it important to make this point, because I don't believe that *Elohim* was used by mistake 2,246 times. Though it is clear that the men God used to write the Scriptures had no concept of the Trinity of God, they were led to use *God* in its plural form *Elohim* rather than one of the other eight Hebrew words used seventy-five percent of the time. It's just one more proof to me that though "penned" by men, the Bible was not "written" by men, but by God. We see in 1 Peter 1:10 that the prophets did not understand what they were being inspired to write about the coming Messiah . . .

1 Peter 1:10: "This salvation was something the prophets did not fully understand. Though they wrote about it, they had many questions as to what it all could mean."

. . . So, also, did they not fully understand about many other things they wrote about—such as the Trinity of God —for it was clear that they followed *one* God. And so do we as Christians follow *one* God.

Once again, I would like to remind you that all the research and study in the world will not prove what man cannot really understand—the mind of God.

Romans 11:34: "*For who among us can know the mind of the Lord?* Who knows enough to be his counselor and guide?" (KJV).

I only know that I believe. When I get to heaven, I will sit at the feet of Jesus and he will explain all of these enigmas of man. For now, I don't need to understand . . . I need only to believe.

Research and study *will* enlarge your knowledge of God in the ways he wants you to know him. The more you know of him, the more you will understand that all of the impossible "stories" in the Bible really can be true. The God I am intimately acquainted with is quite capable of parting a mighty sea, quite able to keep Jonah alive in the belly of that whale for three days, or three years!

Instead of wrestling with the enigmas of God, why not get down to the important business of learning as much about what he has given us to know about him as possible?

He is fascinating! Wouldn't you like to know him better and better?

How Did We Get into This Mess?

How DID MAN fall from grace anyway? It's really a fascinating study. Let's have a peek.

OT   *Genesis 1:1:* "In the beginning God created the heaven and the earth" (KJV).

OT   *Genesis 1:26:* "And God said, Let us make man in our image, after our likeness; and *let them have dominion over the fish of the sea, and over the fowl of the air, and over the cattle, and over all the earth,* and over every creeping thing that creepeth upon the earth" (KJV).

Okay. Here we are told that God created everything and that he gave man dominion over the earth and everything in it!

OT   *Genesis 1:31:* "And God saw everything that he had made, and, behold, *it was very good*" (KJV).

When God created the world, *everything was very good!* There was no evil anywhere.

OT   *Genesis 2:16–17:* "And the Lord God commanded the man, saying, Of every tree of the garden thou mayest freely eat; But of *the tree of the knowledge of good and evil, thou shalt not eat of it; for in the day that thou eatest thereof thou shalt surely die*" (KJV).

Here is the choice . . . without which we would never have been more than mere robots doing the bidding of God. Try having a warm, cozy relationship with a computer and see how you like it!

And with the choice came the warning. God told them they could eat anything in the garden *except* of the tree of knowledge of good and evil! Anything! He also told them if they disobeyed him they "would surely die."

Here's another thought. Doesn't it make sense that if they ate of the fruit of the tree of knowledge of good and evil that they would then experience evil? (They were already experiencing good; see Gen. 1:31.) Evil is what God was protecting them from! Isn't it just the same today? As soon as I go on a diet, I start craving everything fattening that was ever made. Man always wants what he cannot have!

OT *Genesis 2:18:* "And the Lord God said, 'It isn't good for man to be alone; I will make a companion for him, a helper suited to his needs.'"

OT *Genesis 2:21–22:* "Then the Lord God caused the man to fall into a deep sleep, and took one of his ribs and closed up the place from which he had removed it, and made the rib into a woman, and brought her to the man."

. . . And she was named Eve . . . and they lived happily ever after . . . or at least until Eve met the serpent!

OT *Genesis 3:1–4:* "Now the serpent was more subtle than any beast of the field which the Lord God made. And he [the devil] said unto the woman, Yea, hath God said, Ye shall not eat of every tree of the garden? And the woman said unto the serpent, We may eat of the fruit of the trees of the garden; but of the fruit of the tree which is in the midst of the garden, God hath said, Ye shall not eat of it, neither shall ye touch it, lest ye die. And the serpent said unto the woman, *Ye shall not surely die*" (KJV).

Would you listen to Satan? Here he is questioning the authority of God. . . . And causing Eve to question God's authority too. *"Ye shall not surely die."* But isn't that what Satan still does to us today? Hasn't he said that God is so-o-o big that he doesn't really care about our little needs . . . or our little sins? The next time Satan whispers in your ear that a little self-indulgence won't hurt, call him the liar that he is!

John 8:44: ". . . He [Satan] was a murderer from the beginning and a hater of truth—there is not an iota of truth in him. When he lies, it is perfectly normal; for *he is the father of liars.*"

The next time he tells you that the Bible isn't true and that

Jesus isn't the only Way, tell him in the name of Jesus Christ to get out of your life!

In the next Scripture, Satan tells Eve the biggest lie of all—

OT   **Genesis 3:5:** "For God doth know that in the day ye eat thereof, then your eyes shall be opened, and *ye shall be as God,* knowing good and evil" (KJV).

Well! Later we get into who Satan is and where he came from, but for now, suffice it to say that at the time Satan fell from God's good graces in heaven and was eternally exiled, it was just such a thought that started all of *his* troubles. He wanted to "ascend higher than God," and here he is planting the same thought into Eve's mind! (Misery does love company.)

Now we begin to see Eve ponder the temptation. Finally she succumbs completely—a momentous occasion for all mankind.

OT   **Genesis 3:6:** "And when the woman saw that the tree was good for food, and that it was pleasant to the eyes, and *a tree to be desired to make one wise,* she took of the fruit thereof, and did eat, and gave also unto her husband with her; and he did eat" (KJV).

It's interesting that woman always gets the blame for the fall of man, and yet Scripture says it was the sin of *Adam* which caused the fall.

Romans 5:17–18: "The sin of this one man, Adam, caused death to be king over all. . . . Yes, Adam's sin brought punishment to all. . . ."

Why is this? Because it was Adam God commanded not to eat of the tree (Gen. 2:17). Eve was not even created until after that time (Gen. 2:21–22). Eve was "beguiled" by the serpent—tricked.

OT   **Genesis 3:13:** "And the Lord God said unto the woman, What is this that thou has done? And the woman said, *The serpent beguiled me,* and I did eat" (KJV).

Adam knew *exactly* what was going on and yet he went right along with Eve.

OT   **Genesis 3:9–10:** "And the Lord God called unto Adam, and said unto him, Where art thou? And he said, I heard thy voice in the garden, and *I was afraid* . . ." (KJV).

He knew . . . and he was afraid.

I believe the most relevant fact about this study—and I want to emphasize it lest we fail to see it—is that Adam and Eve *disobeyed* God's only command to them. That is still the key to sin. Humans choose to do what God has told them not to do, and not to do what he has told them to do.

One last thought before we move on. The desire for knowledge has always been a problem for man. Satan has always whispered to us that if we are intelligent enough and knowledgeable enough, we won't need God. And a lot of us are "stupid" enough to believe it!

After Adam and Eve ate the fruit . . . after they disobeyed . . . the consequences were immediate.

OT   *Genesis 3:7:* "And the eyes of them both were opened, and they knew that they were naked; and they sewed fig leaves together, and made themselves aprons" (KJV).

And they knew they were naked! Until that very moment, they had lived in total innocence, in their nakedness. But no more. They knew they were naked. Doesn't it make your heart break for what was lost?

OT   *Genesis 3:8:* "And they heard the voice of the Lord God walking in the garden in the cool of the day; and Adam and his wife hid themselves from the presence of the Lord God among the trees of the garden" (KJV).

God actually walked with them every day. And they gave that up to know good and evil. And look at the mess we've been in ever since. I'd hide too, wouldn't you?

OT   *Genesis 3:9:* "And the Lord God called unto Adam, and said unto him, Where art thou?" (KJV).

Don't you imagine that God knew where Adam was and what had happened? Isn't it precious that he didn't come roaring angrily into the Garden and wipe them off the face of the earth? How tenderly God approached them after what they had done.

OT   *Genesis 3:10:* "And he said, I heard thy voice in the garden, and I was afraid, because I was naked; and I hid myself" (KJV).

Wouldn't you be afraid? Adam knew he had made the ultimate boo-boo of all times (and in terms of consequences he had), and yet in the eyes of the "world" today, it was not a monumental sin. It was not murder. It was not adultery. It was not any of those "ugly" sins. It was disobedience . . . pure and simple . . . disobedience. And he knew it meant big trouble for him.

OT **Genesis 3:11:** "And he said, Who told thee that thou was naked? Hast thou eaten of the tree, whereof I commanded thee that thou shouldest not eat?" (KJV).

How gently God handles our humanity! How much he loves us in spite of our frailties and weaknesses!

And yet God had said "they would surely die" if they disobeyed, and God loves with a "tough love." If he says it, he means it. And so mankind began a new and different relationship with him. He no longer walked with Adam and Eve in the Garden. In fact, Adam and Eve were no longer allowed to dwell there.

OT **Genesis 3:23:** "Therefore the Lord God sent him forth from the garden of Eden, to till the ground from where he was taken" (KJV).

Mankind began the new relationship with God of faith.

OT **Habakkuk 2:4:** ". . . Wicked men trust themselves alone, and fail; but the righteous man trusts in me, and lives!"

God began this new relationship by covering their nakedness —the first sign of their disobedience.

OT **Genesis 3:21:** "For Adam also and for his wife did the Lord God make coats of skins, and clothed them" (KJV).

These skins covered their nakedness (the "evidence" of their disobedience) and made them fit for God's presence, just as Christ's righteousness makes us right with God today. (See "God's Righteousness vs. Self-Righteousness—Christ Makes Me Worthy.")

It's rather interesting that after Adam and Eve were confronted with their disobedience that sin began to run rampant!

OT **Genesis 3:12:** "And the man said, *The woman whom thou gavest to be with me, she gave me of the tree, and I did eat*" (KJV).

That's passing the buck! In fact, that's double passing the buck! *You* gave this woman to me, Lord, and *she* made me eat of the tree! It's all her fault!

OT **Genesis 3:13:** "And the Lord God said unto the woman,

What is this that thou has done? And the woman said, *The serpent beguiled me*, and I did eat" (KJV).

It's all the serpent's fault! Yes, women pass the buck too! Sin was already running rampant.

Each blaming the other—how often we see this in our lives today! That's what I love about the Bible. It's current! It's as relevant today as it was when Genesis was first written.

(We see from this sin of Adam and Eve that sin has far-reaching consequences. In a contemporary example, if there is resentment, selfishness, or anger, for example, within a marriage—which is sin—one of the spouses might stray away from the relationship and have an affair. In order to arrange for and cover up this affair, lies have to be told, the family is deprived of valuable time with the parent/spouse, often businesses are "robbed" of work time. Jealousy and suspiciousness rear their ugly heads. Fights ensue. Further consequences could develop. Broken hearts, broken homes, broken children. This is a rather simplistic example of how one sin—resentment, selfishness, or anger—can explode into a multitude of sins and consequences so far-reaching that we couldn't begin to cover it, because statistics regarding children from divorced families reflect that they tend to follow in the same patterns—distrust, anger, resentment, divorce, broken families, and on, and on, and on.)

Now that we have had a look at "how it all happened," we're ready to proceed to the next chapter and find out "The Results of Sin—Why We Need a Savior."

The Results of Sin—Why We Need a Savior—The Wrath of God

SOLID FOOD HAS some bones in it . . . and in this chapter we will take a look (although brief) at the wrathful side of God. Here are a few of those bones to chew on.

OT *Exodus 20:2–5:* "I AM THE LORD THY GOD, WHO HAVE BROUGHT THEE OUT OF THE LAND OF EGYPT, OUT OF THE HOUSE OF BONDAGE. THOU SHALT HAVE NO OTHER GODS BEFORE ME. THOU SHALT NOT MAKE UNTO THEE ANY CARVED IMAGE, OR ANY LIKENESS OF ANYTHING THAT IS IN HEAVEN ABOVE, OR THAT IS IN THE EARTH BENEATH, OR THAT IS IN THE WATER UNDER THE EARTH: THOU SHALT NOT BOW DOWN THYSELF TO THEM, NOR SERVE THEM: FOR I, THE LORD THY GOD, AM A JEALOUS GOD, VISITING THE INIQUITY OF THE FATHERS UPON THE CHILDREN UNTO THE THIRD AND FOURTH GENERATION OF THEM THAT HATE ME" (KJV).

Herein lies the key to God's wrath.

There is only one way ever to understand the wrath of God and that is to draw close to him . . . to know him . . . and to trust him. I can never explain it to you. And let me reassure you that I do not "understand" with any human understanding . . . but with a faith and trust in my God . . . who is just . . . and righteous . . . and loving . . . and long-suffering toward his creatures.

Through in-depth study of the Old Testament I learned these things about him. His patience, tenderness, and mercy toward his children is there on every page. But on those same pages you will see the tribes and nations of people who saw and heard God's love and his warnings to them about their idol-worship and rebellion and continued to disobey.

It was only after generations and generations had failed to heed the warnings that God reached down and destroyed the roots of evil in a community so that he might sow new seeds upon fresh soil. All he ever wanted from them and all he ever wants from us is that we love and worship him—that we have no other gods before us! Yet "modern" man has made idols of many things . . . and I'm not talking about "carved" images. Rather, I am talking about the gods of our contemporary society: money . . . booze . . . drugs . . . gambling . . . celebrities . . . religion . . . philosophy . . . intellect . . . self . . . and so on.

In-depth Bible study reveals that God never proffers a negative without also proffering a positive with which to replace it. He has always given us the choice to love and obey or to rebel and reject. And he has also very carefully told us the results of our choices. Love and obedience bring us into a relationship with him, and a relationship with him brings eternal life and abundant living. Rebellion and rejection bring death. Death is a consequence of his wrath toward unbelievers. I have learned that it is only time spent with him in his word that can give peace and understanding about this difficult subject . . . only he can teach you about these things.

The next verse is God's positive response to the negative proffered in Exodus 20:5.

OT *Exodus 20:6:* "AND SHOWING MERCY UNTO THOUSANDS OF THEM THAT LOVE ME, AND KEEP MY COMMANDMENTS" (KJV).

God is consistent through his Word. There is never a warning without a promise to follow.

Romans 6:23: "For the wages of sin is death [the warning], but the free gift of God is eternal life through Jesus Christ our Lord [the promise]."

OT *Habakkuk 2:4:* "Note this: Wicked men trust themselves alone, and fail [the warning]; but the righteous man trusts in me, and lives [the promise]!"

John 14:6: "Jesus told him, 'I am the Way—yes, and the Truth and the Life [the promise]. No one can get to the Father except by means of me [the warning].'"

1 John 5:11–12: "And what is it that God has said? That he has given us eternal life, and that this life is in his Son [the promise]. So whoever has God's Son has life [the promise]; whoever does not have his Son, does not have life [the warning]."

OT **Psalm 34:15–16:** "For the eyes of the Lord are intently watching all who live good lives [believers], and he gives attention when they cry to him [the promise]. But the Lord has made up his mind to wipe out even the memory of evil men [nonbelievers] from the earth [the warning]."

OT **Psalm 32:10:** "Many sorrows come to the wicked [non-believers] [the warning], but abiding love surrounds those who trust in the Lord [believers]—[the promise]."

Adam and Eve first knew only the beautiful and loving, tender and merciful side of God, yet they didn't believe him or obey him!

OT **Genesis 2:17:** "But of the tree of the knowledge of good and evil, thou shalt not eat of it; for in the day that thou eatest thereof [disobey me] thou shalt surely die" (KJV).

Once again I ask the question I asked earlier. Can you believe those people were so headstrong and rebellious! I don't know anybody like that today, do you? It does seem to be a chronic problem in human nature, doesn't it?

But God has solved our problems!

Romans 3:25: *"For God sent Christ Jesus to take the punishment for our sins and to end all God's anger against us. He used Christ's blood and our faith as the means of saving us from his wrath. In this way he was being entirely fair, even though he did not punish those who sinned in former times. For he was looking forward to the time when Christ would come and take away those sins."*

Romans 5:8–9: "But God showed his great love for us by sending Christ to die for us while we were still sinners. And since by his blood he did all this for us as sinners, how much more will he do for us now that he has declared us not guilty? *Now he will save us from all of God's wrath to come."*

1 John 2:2: "He [Christ] *is the one who took God's wrath against our sins upon himself,* and brought us into fellowship with God; and he is the forgiveness for our sins, and not only ours but all the world's."

1 John 4:10: "In this act we see what real love is: it is not our love for God, but his love for us when *he sent his Son to satisfy God's anger against our sins.*"

OT   *Ezekiel 36:26:* "And I will give you a new heart—I will give you new and right desires—and put a new spirit within you. I will take out your stony hearts of sin and give you new hearts of love."

Eternal life through Jesus Christ . . . peace with God . . . new hearts . . . right desires! Lord . . . You're too much!

Who Is Satan? Where Did He Come From?

NONBELIEVERS AND new believers have little or no concept of Satan and his place in the world. Satan has lulled us into a false sense of security with his cartoon imagery. You know! That little guy in the red suit with horns, tail, and a pitchfork? Well, Jesus referred to that little guy as "a murderer from the beginning, a hater of truth, the father of liars." He has many names and titles. We would do well to examine these so we can recognize him in his many roles.

OTHER NAMES FOR SATAN:

John 8:44: "For you are the children of your father the devil and you love to do the evil things he does. He was *a murderer* from the beginning and *a hater of truth*—there is not an iota of truth in him. When he lies, it is perfectly normal; for he is *the father of liars.*"

2 Corinthians 4:4: "Satan, who is *the god of this evil world . . .*"

2 Corinthians 6:15: "And what concord hath Christ with *Belial?* Or what part hath he that believeth with *an infidel?*" (KJV).

Revelation 9:11: "Their king is the *Prince of the bottomless pit* whose name in Hebrew is *Abaddon,* and in Greek, *Apollyon* [and in English, the *Destroyer*]" (brackets not mine).

2 Corinthians 11:14: "Yet I am not surprised! Satan can change himself into an *angel of light.*"

Luke 10:18: " 'Yes,' he told them, 'I [Jesus] saw *Satan* falling from heaven as a flash of lightning.' "

OT   *Isaiah 14:12:* "How you are fallen from Heaven, O *Lucifer, son of the morning!* How you are cut down to the ground —mighty though you were against the nations of the world."

OT   *Psalm 8:2:* "Out of the mouth of babes and sucklings hast thou ordained strength because of thine enemies, that thou mightest still *the enemy* and *the avenger*" (KJV).

John 17:15: "I pray not that thou shouldest take them out of the world, but that thou shouldest keep them from *the evil*" (KJV).

Matthew 6:13: "Don't bring us into temptation, but deliver us from *the Evil One.* Amen."

1 Peter 5:8: "Be sober, be vigilant, because *your adversary, the devil,* like a roaring lion walketh about seeking whom he may devour" (KJV).

Matthew 12:24: "But when the Pharisees heard about the miracle they said, 'He can cast out demons because he is Satan, *the king of devils.*'"

(The poor Pharisees just could not believe that God would become a man through Jesus Christ. They looked for every excuse to reject him. They even accused him of being Satan himself!)

OT   *Job 15:21:* "A dreadful sound is in his ears; in prosperity *the destroyer* shall come upon him" (KJV).

Revelation 12:10: ". . . for *the Accuser* of our brothers has been thrown down from heaven onto earth—he accused them day and night before our God."

You still may be wondering why we give so much attention to Satan! It's important to know his many names because he is mentioned frequently in Scripture and you need to *know* his names in order to identify him and understand. As you can see from the many references, Satan is God's enemy! He is, therefore, your enemy! Every believer needs to know where his problems are coming from!

Ephesians 6:12: "*For we are not fighting against people made of flesh and blood, but against persons without bodies—the evil rulers of the unseen world, those mighty satanic beings and great evil princes of darkness who rule this world; and against huge numbers of wicked spirits in the spirit world.*"

Where Did Satan Come From?

OT   *Ezekiel 28:14–19:* "*I* [*God*] *appointed you to be the anointed guardian cherub. You had access to the holy mountain of God.* You walked among the stones of fire. You were perfect in all you did from the day you were created until that time when wrong was found in you. Your great wealth filled you with internal turmoil and you sinned. *Therefore, I cast you out of the mountain of God like a common sinner. I destroyed you,* O overshadowing cherub, from the midst of the stones of fire. *Your heart was filled with pride because of all your beauty; you corrupted your wisdom for the sake of your splendor. Therefore I have cast you down to the ground* and exposed you helpless before the curious gaze of kings. *You defiled your holiness with lust for gain; therefore, I brought forth fire from your own actions and let it burn you to ashes upon the earth in the sight of all those watching you.* All who know you are appalled at your fate; *you are an example of horror; you are destroyed forever.*"

We see from the above Scripture that Satan was once *the* anointed cherub of God. He was special! . . . But he blew it! His heart "was filled with pride because of his beauty; his wisdom was corrupted for the sake of his splendor . . . his holiness was defiled by lust for gain." Satan had the best of everything, just like Adam and Eve! And just like Adam and Eve, he blew the whole deal!

The saga continues—

OT   *Isaiah 14:12–14:* "How you are fallen from heaven, O Lucifer, son of the morning! How you are cut down to the ground—mighty though you were against the nations of the world. For you said to yourself, '*I will ascend to heaven and rule the angels. I will take the highest throne. I will preside on the Mount of Assembly far away in the north. I will climb to the highest heavens and be like the Most High.*'"

Notice that Lucifer used the word *I* four times in four sentences! When Lucifer uttered the first *I*, sin began. But to say he will be like the Most High! Oh, my!

Do you remember in Genesis 3:5 that Satan tempted Eve

with the same thought? He told her she would be as God if she would eat of the fruit of the tree of knowledge of good and evil. The very same sin that got him kicked out of heaven! Poor Eve! Poor Adam! . . . Poor mankind! Instead of becoming like God, we came under the dominion of Satan and became slaves to sin. Adam lost the dominion given man over this world to Satan—who then took the title Prince of this world.

Don't despair, though! God has a positive to replace this negative, remember?

John 12:31: "The time of judgment for the world has come [this is Jesus speaking]—and the time when Satan, *the prince of this world,* shall be cast out."

As a side note here, the "judgment" referred to in this verse relates to Jesus Christ as the bearer of the believer's sins which have been nailed to the Cross with him. The believer is justified through the death of our Lord, Jesus Christ. Praise the Lord! This is the only judgment the believer will face.

John 5:24: "Verily, verily, I say unto you, he that heareth my Word, and believeth on him that sent me, hath everlasting life, and *shall not come into judgment,* but is passed from death unto life" (KJV).

But most importantly, please note that the prince of this world was cast out at the time of Jesus' crucifixion and resurrection. That means Satan is no longer the prince of this world. Jesus now reigns as King of kings and Lord of lords and we, as believers, are to reign with him.

Ephesians 1:18–23: "The eyes of your understanding being enlightened; that ye may know what is the hope of his calling, and what the riches of the glory of *his inheritance in the saints,* and what is the exceeding greatness of his power toward us who believe, according to the working of his mighty power, which he wrought in Christ, when he raised him from the dead, *and set him at his own right hand in the heavenly places,* far above all principality, and power, and might, and dominion, and every name that is named, not only in this world, but also in that which is to come; *and hath put all things under his feet,* and gave him to be the head over all things to the church, which is his body, the fulness of him that filleth all in all" (KJV).

Ephesians 2:6: "*And hath raised us up together in heavenly places* in Christ Jesus" (KJV).

John 3:16: "For God so loved the world, that he gave his only begotten Son, that *whosoever believeth in him should not perish, but have everlasting life*" (KJV).

At this point you may be asking the same questions I was asking. Why would God allow this to happen? Why can't he just make us all perfect like him?

Earlier we considered what it would be like to be loved by a doll that said, "I love you," every time you pulled the string. Here is another example of that same problem. Can you imagine loving a robot? There certainly would be no spontaneity in that kind of love. It wouldn't be a delight to the Lord the way it is when we spontaneously fall on our knees and love and adore him. Not only does it thrill and delight him, but I feel sure the angels must burst forth into song and the heavens must fill with glory to him. After all, he is God; he deserves that kind of love. He deserves to have us choose him; he is our Creator.

Satan had that same choice. God gave Adam and Eve that same option. But we can't have it both ways. It's God's way or nothing. God's way is to choose him through his Son, Jesus Christ. If you haven't, won't you choose him now? He is waiting so patiently . . . but with great anticipation, just for you!

So much for the negative world of Satan. We see from John 12:31 that Jesus Christ won the victory over Satan . . . so let's move on to examine that in greater depth.

Jesus Won the Victory over Satan

Romans 5:12: "*When Adam sinned, sin entered the entire human race.* His sin spread death throughout all the world, so everything began to grow old and die, *for all sinned.*"

Jesus Christ was born without the blemish of original sin. He was born of a virgin, conceived by the Holy Spirit—God himself.

Luke 1:28–38: "And the angel came in unto her, and said, Hail, thou that art highly favoured, the Lord is with thee: blessed art thou among women. And when she saw him, she was troubled at his saying, and cast in her mind what manner of salutation this should be. And the angel said unto her, Fear not, Mary: for thou has found favour with God. And, behold, thou shalt conceive in thy womb, and bring forth a son, and shalt call his name Jesus. He shall be great, and shall be called the Son of the Highest: and the Lord God shall give unto him the throne of his father David: And he shall reign over the house of Jacob for ever; and of his kingdom there shall be no end. Then said Mary unto the angel, How shall this be, seeing *I know not a man?* And the angel answered and said unto her, *The Holy Ghost shall come upon thee,* and the power of the Highest shall overshadow thee: therefore also that holy thing which shall be born of thee shall be called the Son of God. And, behold, thy cousin Elisabeth, she hath also conceived a son in her old age: and this is the sixth month with her, who was called barren. For with God nothing shall be impossible. And Mary said, Behold the handmaid of the Lord; be it unto me according to thy word. And the angel departed from her" (KJV).

The virgin birth is one of the great mysteries of God. I do not claim to understand it, but I do believe it. Without the virgin birth, all of Christianity would be a farce. The virgin birth was *prophesied* in the Old Testament:

OT   *Isaiah 7:14:* "Therefore, the Lord himself shall give you a sign; Behold, a virgin shall conceive, and bear a son, and shall call his name Immanuel [translates 'God is with us']" (KJV).

When Jesus Christ died on the cross at Calvary and was resurrected, he defeated Satan and death; not for himself, because he was without sin—but for you, and for me. Jesus was the perfect and ultimate sacrifice. He was the "Lamb without blemish."

John 1:29: "The next day John saw Jesus coming toward him and said, 'Look! There is *the Lamb of God who takes away the world's sin!*' "

1 Peter 1:19: "But he [God] paid for you with the precious lifeblood of *Christ, the sinless, spotless Lamb of God.*"

To more fully understand the "perfect sacrifice" of Jesus Christ, we can, by looking through the blood sacrifices of the Old Testament, which were used to atone for sin (something we will study in greater depth in the next chapter), see that the one requirement for every sacrifice was that the animal be perfect . . . without blemish. To give you just a few examples—

OT   *Leviticus 3:1:* "And if his oblation be a sacrifice of peace offering, if he offer it of the herd; whether it be a male or female, he shall offer it *without blemish* before the Lord" (KJV).

OT   *Leviticus 3:6:* "And if his offering for a sacrifice of peace offering unto the Lord be of the flock; male or female, he shall offer it *without blemish*" (KJV).

OT   *Leviticus 4:3:* "If the priest that is anointed do sin according to the sin of the people; then let him bring for his sin, which he hath sinned, a young bullock *without blemish* unto the Lord for a sin offering" (KJV).

In each of the above Scriptures, the animal sacrificed was to be perfect, without blemish.

And so we begin to get a picture of how the perfect sacrifice, Jesus Christ, won the victory over Satan and death. We do not have to fear Satan.

Hebrews 2:14: "Since we, God's children, are human beings —made of flesh and blood—he became flesh and blood too by being born in human form; for *only as a human being could he die and in dying break the power of the devil who had the power of death.*"

Colossians 2:14–15: "And [God] blotted out the charges proved against you, the list of his commandments which you had not obeyed. He took this list of sins and destroyed it by nailing it to Christ's cross. *In this way God took away Satan's power to accuse you of sin, and God openly displayed to the whole world Christ's triumph at the cross where your sins were all taken away.*"

1 John 3:8: ". . . But *the Son of God came to destroy these works of the devil.*"

2 Corinthians 5:21: "For God took the sinless Christ and poured into him our sins. Then, in exchange, he poured God's goodness into us!"

Now, that's love.

1 John 4:4: "Dear young friends, you belong to God and have already won your fight with those who are against Christ, because *there is someone in your hearts who is stronger than any evil teacher in this wicked world.*"

Luke 10:19: "And I have given you [believers] authority over all the power of the enemy, and to walk among serpents and scorpions and to crush them. *Nothing shall injure you.*"

1 Corinthians 15:55: "O death, where then your victory? Where then your sting? For sin—the sting that causes death—will all be gone; and the law, which reveals our sins, will no longer be our judge."

It's important to understand that with Jesus Christ as our Savior, Satan is powerless. He tries to harass us, and occasionally we allow him to get away with it, but it is clearly stated that Jesus defeated Satan on the cross at Calvary. God *is* in control!

Luke 12:32: "*So don't be afraid, little flock.* For it gives your Father great happiness to give you the Kingdom."

John 10:11: "I am the Good Shepherd. The Good Shepherd lays down his life for the sheep."

John 10:27–29: "My sheep recognize my voice, and I know them, and they follow me. I give them eternal life and they shall never perish. *No one shall snatch them away from me, for my Father has given them to me, and he is more powerful than anyone else, so no one can kidnap them from me.*"

One last thought before we continue. The next two Scriptures are given to reveal to us that, even though Jesus died a physical death, *no one,* not even Satan, can take the life of God. Jesus chose to give up his life that we might be redeemed.

John 10:17–18: "The Father loves me because I lay down my life that I may have it back again. *No one can kill me without my consent—I lay down my life voluntarily.* For I have the right and power to lay it down when I want to and also the right and power to take it again. For the Father has given me this right."

John 19:30: "When Jesus had tasted it, he said, 'It is finished,' and *bowed his head and dismissed his Spirit.*"

Thank you, dear Jesus!

This chapter is a perfect prologue to the next chapter, "Why Did Jesus Have to Die?"

Why Did Jesus Have to Die?

OT *Leviticus 17:11:* "*For the life of the flesh is in the blood,* and I have given you the blood to sprinkle upon the altar as an atonement for your souls; *it is the blood that makes atonement, because it is the life.*"

Hebrews 9:22: "In fact we can say that under the old agreement [the Levitical law] almost everything was cleansed by sprinkling it with blood, and *without the shedding of blood there is no forgiveness of sins.*"

I did not understand for such a long time after I became a believer why Jesus Christ had to die. It was not a question that weighed heavily on my mind, but rather it was one that existed in a "fuzzy" way in the back of my mind. Couldn't God have found a better way than having his precious Son die?

The answer to this question is the very essence of the Bible . . . it is the very essence of faith. Do you remember when God warned Adam and Eve that they would surely die if they ate of the tree of knowledge of good and evil?

Well, we learned that they *did* eat and they *did* fall from Grace. The death God warned them about was a spiritual death. The penalty for disobedience to God is spiritual death.

Christ had to die . . . He had to shed his precious blood . . . so that he, by substituting himself for the world, could defeat this spiritual death *for us.* And how did he do that? By his death and resurrection!

This substitutionary death was not something God whimsically devised (God does nothing whimsical). He

191

had, through the Levitical Laws of sacrifice thousands of years before Christ's sacrifice, given the Jews the substitutionary death of animals as a provision for their sins until the Promised One, the Messiah, would come to save them once and for all, for the animal sacrifices had to be made every year.

The purpose of the shedding of blood in animal sacrifices was that it represented to the sacrificer (sinner) that a *substitute* had died in his or her place . . . because the natural consequence of sin is spiritual death. (Remember, God told Adam that if he ate from the Tree of Knowledge of Good and Evil he would surely die.) Thus, in the sacrifice of an animal the sacrificer could see the effects of sin and transgression in his or her life and be warned about them. Sacrifice imparted the message that sin is the cause of death and also served to show that through faith in God-ordained sacrifice, a substitute could be put to death in order to atone for, or cleanse, sin.

The blood sacrifices of animals in the Old Testament were only "pictures" of the ultimate, the final, sacrifice— Jesus Christ the Son of God.

We're now going to look at a few of the significant incidences of sacrifice in the Old Testament in order to enlarge our understanding of the sacrificial death of Jesus.

The first sacrifice in the Bible is in the third chapter of Genesis. After Adam and Eve disobeyed God and ate from the tree of knowledge of good and evil, they were immediately aware of their own nakedness and tried to cover themselves—rather inadequately.

 OT *Genesis 3:7:* "And as they ate it, suddenly they became aware of their nakedness, and were embarrassed. So they strung fig leaves together to cover themselves around the hips."

The Lord is so merciful to his children. He has never left us to die in our sin and disobedience without providing a way out. He saw that Adam and Eve were truly grieved by their sin, that they were repentant, and he made provisions for the covering of their nakedness—their sin.

The fig leaves were not suitable to the Lord. The fig leaves were a perfect picture of man trying to make himself right (self-righteousness). As has always been true, God provided the suitable covering.

OT **Genesis 3:21:** "And the Lord God clothed Adam and his wife with garments made from the skins of animals."

This was not, at that time in Scripture, specifically referred to as a blood sacrifice, but obviously animals had to be slain (blood had to be shed) in order to obtain the coats of fur to cover their nakedness.

This coat of skin is a "type" of Christ. It covered the sins of the wearers and symbolizes the righteousness of the coming Messiah. Even though Christ had not yet been born as man, this was God's way of "saving" his children. *Today, we are saved by the same righteousness of Christ.* (We are going to cover "types of Christ" chapter-after-next, so don't let that term worry you.)

1 Corinthians 1:30: "For it is from God alone that you have your life through Christ Jesus. He showed us God's plan of salvation; *he was the one who made us acceptable to God; he made us pure and holy and gave himself to purchase our salvation [with his blood].*"

Christ died for our sins. His blood was shed.

Ephesians 1:7: "*In whom we have redemption through his blood,* the forgiveness of sins, according to the riches of his grace" (KJV).

The coats of skins were garments of righteousness to cover the nakedness of Adam and Eve. They were provided by God that the first sinners might be made acceptable for the presence of God.

OT **Isaiah 61:10:** "Let me tell you how happy God has made me! For he has clothed me with *garments of salvation* and draped about me the *robe of righteousness.* I am like a bridegroom in his wedding suit or a bride with her jewels."

The second occasion for sacrifice was Cain and Abel. This is where Cain lost his soul. Let's see why.

OT **Genesis 4:3–5:** "At harvest time Cain brought the Lord a gift of his farm produce, and Abel brought the fatty cuts of meat from his best lambs, and presented them to the Lord. And the Lord accepted Abel's offering, but not Cain's. This made Cain both dejected and very angry, and his face grew dark with fury."

Cain's sacrifice was not a blood sacrifice. His was "fruit of the ground." This "fruit of the ground" sacrifice was based on his own "good works" and not upon the obedience which God requires. Without the shedding of blood, there is no remission of our sins.

Hebrews 9:22: "In fact we can say that under the old agreement almost everything was cleansed by sprinkling it with blood, and *without the shedding of blood there is no forgiveness of sins.*"

But Abel was obedient, and the Lord accepted his offering.

Hebrews 11:4: "*It was by faith that Abel obeyed God and brought an offering that pleased God more than Cain's offering did.* God accepted Abel and proved it by accepting his gift; and *though Abel is long dead, we can still learn lessons from him about trusting God.*"

Abel's offering, the lamb, is a "type" of Christ too—the Lamb of God. A lamb fitly symbolizes the unresisting innocency and harmlessness of the Lord Jesus Christ. Jesus was the Lamb of God.

John 1:29: "The next day John [the Baptist] saw Jesus coming toward him and said, 'Look! *There is the Lamb of God who takes away the world's sins.*'"

But God gave Cain one more chance to make the proper offering.

OT *Genesis 4:7:* "*It can be bright with joy [Cain] if you will do what you should!* But if you refuse to obey, watch out. Sin is waiting to attack you, longing to destroy you. But you can conquer it!"—[by obeying].

But what was Cain's response? It was not obedience.

OT *Genesis 4:8:* "One day Cain suggested to his brother, 'Let's go out into the fields.' And while they were together there, Cain attacked and killed his brother."

He killed his own brother! God offered him another chance and he rejected it. I say to myself that I cannot believe Cain could be so rebellious and disobedient . . . and with God speaking directly to him! Yet I know that I, too, am rebellious. It took me thirty-six years to accept the blood sacrifice of Jesus Christ as the payment for that rebelliousness and disobedience in me. (Many people never accept it.)

The story about Abraham and Isaac is perhaps the clearest

picture of God the Father and his Son Jesus Christ there is in the Bible. Later, in the chapter, "Why Are the Jews God's Chosen Ones?" we will study in depth about Abraham and Isaac. You will learn that Isaac was not conceived by Abraham until he was over 100 years old—an incredible miracle (all miracles are incredible). You will also learn that it was through Isaac that God would make Abraham the father of many nations and through whom all the families of the world would be blessed. All of these facts precede and are given as background to bring you to a point in Abraham's life when God asked an incredible thing of him—

OT *Genesis 22:1–2:* "Later on, God tested Abraham's [faith and obedience]. 'Abraham!' God called. 'Yes, Lord?' he replied. 'Take with you your only son—yes, Isaac whom you love so much—and go to the land of Moriah and *sacrifice him* there as a burnt offering upon one of the mountains which I'll point out to you!' "

. . . Here was Abraham with his beloved son, Isaac, *the seed* through whom the world was to be blessed . . . and here was God, asking Abraham to sacrifice Isaac on an altar.

But Abraham trusted God and, therefore, he was able to obey God, even with a request as tough as this one.

OT *Genesis 22:6:* "Abraham placed the wood for the burnt offering upon Isaac's shoulders, while he himself carried the knife and the flint for striking a fire. So the two of them went on together."

In the next verses, you will see an eye-opening statement.

OT *Genesis 22:7–8:* "And Isaac spake unto Abraham his father, and said, My father: and he said, Here am I, my son. And he said, Behold the fire and the wood: but where is the lamb for a burnt offering? And Abraham said, My son, *God will provide **himself** a lamb for a burnt offering:* so they went both of them together" (KJV).

Has that phrase in italics sunken in? Has the Holy Spirit nudged you? This is Genesis! the first book of the Bible! Here we see the "picture" of Jesus Christ, the Messiah, the Lamb of God, *God himself,* unfolding! Jesus *himself* was the lamb God provided.

John 1:29: "The next day John (the Baptist) saw Jesus

coming toward him and said, 'Look! There is *the Lamb of God* who takes away the world's sins.' "

Let's continue the saga of Abraham and Isaac—

OT *Genesis 22:9:* "When they arrived at the place where God had told Abraham to go, he built an altar and placed the wood in order, ready for the fire, and then tied Isaac and laid him on the altar over the wood."

Notice here that Isaac was no longer a "little one," as he spoke with his father as a young man and he was strong enough to carry the firewood upon his shoulders; and yet he obediently and willingly allowed himself to be placed on the altar for sacrifice. There is not a hint of a struggle, just as Jesus Christ obediently and willingly sacrificed himself for the sins of the world.

OT *Isaiah 53:7:* "He was oppressed and he was afflicted, yet *he never said a word.* He was brought as a lamb to the slaughter; and as a sheep before her shearers is dumb, so *he stood silent* before the ones condemning him."

Matthew 27:12-14: "But when the chief priests and other Jewish leaders made their many accusations against him, *Jesus remained silent.* 'Don't you hear what they are saying?' Pilate demanded. But *Jesus said nothing,* much to the governor's surprise."

Genesis 22:9 states that Isaac was bound (tied) and yet there was no struggle indicated. Jesus was nailed to the cross without a trace of resistance. In fact, just as Isaac carried the wood for the fire that was to be burned for his own sacrifice (Gen. 22:6), so did Jesus carry his own cross (hewn from a tree) to his place of crucifixion (sacrifice).

John 19:17-18: "So they had him at last, and he was taken out of the city, carrying his cross to the place known as 'The Skull,' in Hebrew, 'Golgotha.' There they crucified him. . . ."

Abraham loved and trusted God so much that he was willing to sacrifice his beloved son, Isaac, for whom he had longed and waited and agonized until he was over 100 years old!

OT *Genesis 22:10:* "And Abraham took the knife and lifted it up to plunge it into his son, to slay him."

And God honored that love and trust.

OT *Genesis 22:11-12:* "At that moment the Angel of God

shouted to him from heaven, 'Abraham! Abraham!' 'Yes, Lord!' he answered. 'Lay down the knife; don't hurt the lad in any way,' the Angel said, 'for I know that God is first in your life—you have not withheld even your beloved son from me.'"

We have in this study of Abraham and Isaac something so rich it is almost incomprehensible. We have (1) a lesson on what it means to trust God, for you will learn in the in-depth study of Abraham how God blessed him for his obedience and faith; and just as God demonstrated to Abraham that he could be trusted with his precious son, so also does God demonstrate to us that he can be trusted with our selves—our burdens and woes. Yes, he can be trusted with our problem spouses, parents, children and friends. And we are called to put all of those onto the altar for him to deal with. But I remind you once again, because it cannot be said often enough, God can be trusted! (2) We have another example of how perfect God's Bible is! The Old Testament is basically a "picture" of what was and is to come. The New Testament fulfilled much of the Old Testament with the life, death, and resurrection of Jesus Christ; though there will be complete fulfillment with the second coming of Christ. In Abraham we have a "picture" or "type" of God the Father, in that he was willing to sacrifice his son. In Isaac we have a "picture" or "type" of Christ, in that he was willing to be sacrificed. In a later chapter, "Types and Shadows of Christ in the Old Testament," we will look at the Old Testament in greater depth from this perspective.

But we are not yet through with this sacrifice study—

OT *Genesis 22:13–14:* "Then Abraham noticed a ram caught by its horns in a bush. So he took the ram and sacrificed it, instead of his son, as a burnt offering on the altar. Abraham named the place 'Jehovah provides'—and it still goes by that name to this day."

These two verses are also very rich. God provided a substitute sacrifice for Isaac. Thus the ram in this case was a "type" of Christ, in that it was a substitute, just as Christ was sacrificed for us (substituted—in our place) that we might have eternal life.

Romans 3:25: "For God sent Christ Jesus to take the punishment for our sins and to end all God's anger against us. . . ."

Another interesting thing about Genesis 22:14 is that Abraham named the place where all this occurred "Jehovah-jireh," which translates, "God provides." The Hebrew word for *Jesus* is *Jehoshua,* which translates "God saves."

It's so beautiful my heart feels as if it may burst!

I suppose one of the clearest pictures of deliverance from death through the blood sacrifice is the Passover. The Lord Jehovah had warned the Pharaoh time and time again that he and his people were in danger of his wrath because of their idol-worship and debauchery, and especially their persecution of the Jews—his chosen ones. (See Exodus; that is what chapters 3 through 11 are all about.) But, finally, after Pharaoh failed to heed his warnings, the Lord's wrath fell upon him and the Egyptians.

OT   *Exodus 12:12:* "For I will pass through the land of Egypt tonight and kill all the oldest sons and firstborn male animals in all the land of Egypt, and execute judgment upon all the gods of Egypt—for I am Jehovah."

Don't forget, the Israelites also lived in Egypt. So God made provision for their protection through the blood sacrifice.

OT   *Exodus 12:2–7:* "From now on, this month will be the first and most important month of the Jewish calendar. Annually, on the tenth day of this month (announce this to all the people of Israel) each family shall get a lamb (or, if a family is small, let it share the lamb with another small family in the neighborhood; whether to share in this way depends on the size of the families). This animal shall be a year-old male, either a sheep or a goat, without any defects. On the evening of the fourteenth day of this month, all *these lambs shall be killed, and their blood shall be placed on the two side-frames of the door of every home and on the panel above the door. Use the blood of the lamb eaten in that home.*"

OT   *Exodus 12:11:* ". . . This observance shall be called the Lord's Passover."

OT   *Exodus 12:13: "The blood you have placed on the doorposts will be proof that you obey me,* and when I see the blood

I will *pass over* you and I will not destroy your firstborn children when I smite the land of Egypt."

In this Scripture we see that the Israelites were saved because of their *obedience to God* . . . The blood on the doorposts proved that a lamb had already died as a substitute for the members of the household. Since the penalty of death had been paid by a God-ordained sacrifice, those within the household were protected from death.

Once again, we are given a picture of the Lamb of God who takes away the sins of the world (John 1:29). Death "passes over" those who believe.

It's such a pity to have to leave the Passover here, because it is a rich study for believers. Many churches today offer studies in all of the Jewish feasts throughout the year. If you search around you will find one. It's worth the effort.

When Moses received the Law from God upon the Mount, God provided in that body of law not only the Ten Commandments but laws for living. An important part of that Law was the provision for sacrifices.

OT *Exodus 20:24:* "The altars you make for me must be simple altars of earth. *Offer upon them your sacrifices to me—* your burnt offerings and peace offerings of sheep and oxen. Build altars only where I tell you to, and I will come and bless you there."

OT *Leviticus 17:11:* "For the life of the flesh is in the blood, and I have given you the blood to sprinkle upon the altar as an atonement for your souls; *it is the blood that makes atonement, because it is the life.*"

OT *Leviticus 16:29–30:* "This is a permanent law: You must do no work on the twenty-fifth day of September, but must spend the day in self-examination and humility. This applies whether you are born in the land or are a foreigner living among the people of Israel; for *this is the day commemorating the atonement, cleansing you in the Lord's eyes from all of your sins.*"

Atonement translates "covering." Therefore, the Old Testament sacrifices never removed man's sin. In other words, the sacrifices merely covered the offerer's sin and secured the divine forgiveness of the Lord.

Hebrews 10:1: "The old system of Jewish laws gave only a

dim foretaste of the good things Christ would do for us. The sacrifices under the old system were repeated again and again, year after year, but *even so they could never save those who lived under their rules.*"

These Old Testament sins, which God "passed over," were never vindicated until Jesus Christ died on the cross, a propitiation for the sins of the whole world.

Romans 3:25: *"For God sent Christ Jesus to take the punishment for our sins and to end all God's anger against us.* He used Christ's blood and our faith as the means of saving us from his wrath. In this way he was being entirely fair, even though *he did not punish those who sinned in former times. For he was looking forward to the time when Christ would come and take away those sins."*

The people in the Old Testament were saved just as we of the New Testament are saved—by faith. The blood sacrifices evidenced their faith.

OT   *Isaiah 45:22:* "Look unto me and be saved, all the ends of the earth; for I am God, and there is none else" (KJV).

Hebrews 9:9–15: "This has an important lesson for us today. For under the old system, gifts and sacrifices were offered, but these failed to cleanse the hearts of the people who brought them. For the old system dealt only with certain rituals—what foods to eat and drink, rules for washing themselves, and rules about this and that. *The people had to keep these rules to tide them over until Christ came with God's new and better way.* He came as High Priest of this better system which we now have. He went into that greater, perfect tabernacle in heaven, not made by men nor part of this world, and once for all took blood into that inner room, the Holy of Holies, and sprinkled it on the mercy seat; but it was not the blood of goats and calves. *No, he took his own blood, and with it he, by himself, made sure of our eternal salvation. And if under the old system the blood of bulls and goats and the ashes of young cows could cleanse men's bodies from sin, just think how much more surely the blood of Christ will transform our lives and hearts.* His sacrifice frees us from the worry of having to obey the old rules, and makes us want to serve the living God. For by the help of the eternal Holy

Spirit, Christ willingly gave himself to God to die for our sins—he being perfect, without a single sin or fault. Christ came with this new agreement so that all who are invited may come and have forever all the wonders God has promised them. *For Christ died to rescue them from the penalty of the sins they had committed while still under the old system."*

Colossians 1:20–22: "It was through what his Son did that God cleared a path for everything to come to him—all things in heaven and on earth—for Christ's death on the cross has made peace with God for all by his blood." This includes you who were once so far away from God. You were his enemies and hated him and were separated from him by your evil thoughts and actions, yet now he has brought you back as his friends. He has done this through the death on the cross of his own human body, and now as a result Christ has brought you into the very presence of God, and you are standing there before him with nothing left against you—nothing left that he could even chide you for."

Jesus Christ was the perfect sacrifice, the perfect offering. (He voluntarily "offered" up his own life.)

*John 10:18: "*No man can kill me without my consent— *I lay down [offer] my life voluntarily.* For I have the right and power to lay it down when I want to and also the right and power to take it again. For the Father has given me this right."

So we see from this study that it was Jesus' death on the cross, not the Levitical animal sacrifices, which made full and complete redemption. The Old Testament sacrifices enabled God to go on with a guilty people because those sacrifices "typified" the death of Jesus on the cross. To the offerer, they were the confession of his sinful nature and expression of his faith. To God, they were the "shadows" of good things that were to come, of which Jesus Christ was the reality.

*Hebrews 10:1: "*For the law *having a shadow of good things to come,* and not the very image of the things, can never with those sacrifices which they offered year by year continually make the comers thereunto perfect" (KJV).

In this profound chapter we have before us as clearly as can be written a perfect picture of why salvation is a result of what *God did* . . . not what man does.

Ephesians 2:8–9: "Because of his kindness you have been saved through trusting Christ. And even trusting is not of yourselves; it too is a gift from God. Salvation is not a reward for the good we have done, so *none of us can take any credit for it.*"

Also, we see the difference between Christianity and all other religions of the world. In other religions, man reaches (and reaches, and reaches) up to God, but in Christianity God reached down to man through his son Jesus Christ, and he sent his Holy Spirit, the Spirit of God himself, to indwell each believer.

Toward the end of his life, Mahatma Gandhi, the devoted Hindu leader, wrote that he felt miserably and tortuously far away from God. How sad!

A person who sincerely invites Jesus Christ into his heart will *know* he is there, will feel his touch! Because Jesus Christ defeated death by his resurrection and he lives today. Our God lives!

Revelation 1:18: "I am he that liveth, and was dead; and, behold, I am alive for evermore . . ." (KJV).

Our responsibility is to accept the sacrifice of Jesus Christ; accept that he died in our place and praise him with great thanksgiving for his love. Henceforth, we are under his grace. (Remember the definition of grace?—the divine influence upon the heart that manifests itself in the life.)

OT *Song of Solomon 8:7:* "Many waters cannot quench the flame of love, neither can the floods drown it. If a man tried to buy it with everything he owned, he couldn't do it."

Rom. 8:38–39: "For I am persuaded that neither death, nor life, nor [evil] angels, nor principalities, nor powers, nor things present, nor things to come, nor height, nor depth, nor any other creation, shall be able to separate us from the love of God, which is in Christ Jesus, our Lord" (KJV).

Why Are the Jews God's Chosen Ones?

OT *Deuteronomy 7:6:* "For thou art an holy people unto the
Lord thy God: the Lord thy God hath chosen thee to be
a special people unto himself, above all people that are
upon the face of the earth" (KJV).

THIS IS A question which puzzled me, and I am sure most
people . . . so let's devote a little time to it. It is not only
an important issue for Jews. It is essential to Christians.

Why *did* God choose the Jews as his "chosen people?" In
seeking the answer, we must look back to the time when
there were no "Jews." It was not the "Jews," per se, who
were the "chosen"; it was, rather, the "seed" of Abraham,
the "father of many nations."

OT *Genesis 12:1–3:* "After the death of Abram's [later to be
named Abraham] father, God told him, 'Leave your own
country behind you, and your own people, and go to the
land I will guide you to. *If you do, I will cause you to become the father of a great nation;* I will bless you and
make your name famous, and *you will be a blessing to
many others.* I will bless those who bless you and curse
those who curse you; and the entire world will be blessed
because of you.'"

This blessing of the entire world culminated with the birth
of Jesus Christ.

We can see through the genealogy of Mary (Luke 3:23–
38), that Jesus Christ did come from the "seed" of Abraham.

At the time of Genesis 12:1–3, the covenant had not yet
been made, because there were conditions that had not yet
been met. God told Abram that he had to "leave his country
behind him and go where he led him" and that *if* he obeyed

that command he would "become the father of a great nation."

And so Abram began the walk of faith . . . believing and obeying God.

OT   *Genesis 12:4:* "So Abram departed as the Lord had instructed him, and Lot went too; Abram was seventy-five years old at that time."

Abram left his home and family to move as God led him . . . at the incredible age of seventy-five! That in itself is a real step of faith. But as we consider this verse further, we must remember the promise that Abram would become the *father* of a great nation . . . but he and his wife Sarai, at that time, had no children!

OT   *Genesis 11:30:* "But Sarai [later to be named Sarah] was barren; she had no children."

This meant that he would have to bear a "seed" of his own in order to be the "father of a great nation." Sarai was sixty-five, long past the child-bearing age, and Abram was no spring chicken! Now that really did require faith . . . and Abram believed . . . for awhile. After all, it had been (as best I can tell) about ten years since the Lord had given Abram the "promise of the promise," and Abram wasn't getting any younger. So he cried out to the Lord.

OT   *Genesis 15:1-2:* "Afterwards Jehovah spoke to Abram in a vision, and this is what he told him: 'Don't be fearful, Abram, for I will defend you. And I will give you great blessings.' But Abram replied, '*O Lord Jehovah, what good are all your blessings when I have no son?*'"

Let's look at it from Abram's perspective. He had been obedient to God's command and had left his home and family and endured many trials during that time. Yet he still was not a "father."

But God comforted and reassured Abram.

OT   *Genesis 15:4:* "Then Jehovah told him, 'No, no one else will be your [adopted] heir, for you *will* have a son [of your own] to inherit everything you own.'"

And so Abram believed God when he promised Abram a child from his own seed!

OT   *Genesis 15:6:* "And *Abram believed God; then God considered him righteous on account of his faith.*"

But Sarai's faith began to erode. After all, she was seventy-five (or so) years old! And it *was* Abram to whom God had made the promise. It wasn't that she doubted God; she just wasn't sure she was included!

OT **Genesis 16:1–4:** "But Sarai and Abram had no children. So Sarai took her maid, an Egyptian girl named Hagar, and gave her to Abram to be his second wife. 'Since the Lord has given me no children,' Sarai said, 'you may sleep with my servant girl, and her children shall be mine.' And Abram agreed. (This took place ten years after Abram had first arrived in the land of Canaan.) So he slept with Hagar, and she conceived. . . ." (Parentheses not mine.)

It's very interesting to see the translation of Sarai's name in relation to this situation. *Sarai* translates "dominative." Here Sarai pushed Abram into the bed of Hagar, fully acting out her name!

And she recognized this sin and disbelief as hers.

OT **Genesis 16:5:** "Then Sarai said to Abram, May [the responsibility for] *my* wrong and deprivation of rights be upon you!" (*Amplified Bible,* brackets not mine).

Sarai knew it was her wrong, and God knew it was her disbelief. But a child was conceived and born to Hagar out of this disbelief.

OT **Genesis 16:15–16:** "So Hagar gave Abram a son, and Abram named him Ishmael. (Abram was eighty-six years old at this time.)"

But Ishmael was not the son God had promised. Ishmael was born out of direct disobedience to God, brought on by Sarai's disbelief in what God promised. (Adam and Eve fell because of disbelief. Once again we see that disbelief and the resulting disobedience are a chronic problem with man!)

But God's mercy is long-suffering toward his creatures. He understands our problem. God had a plan and that plan was that Jesus Christ would be born out of the seed of Abraham, and he never lost sight of that plan. (God can be counted on never to lose sight of his plan . . . and that includes the ones he has for each of us.)

OT **Genesis 17:1–8:** "When Abram was ninety-nine years old, God appeared to him and told him, 'I am the Almighty; obey me and live as you should. I will prepare a contract

[the promise confirmed] between us, guaranteeing to
make you into a mighty nation. In fact you shall be the
father of not only one nation, but *a multitude of nations!*
Abram fell face downward in the dust as God talked with
him. 'What's more,' God told him, 'I am changing your
name. It is no longer "Abram" ("Exalted Father") but
"Abraham" ("Father of Nations")—for that is what you
will be. I have declared it. I will give you millions of
descendants who will form many nations! *Kings shall be
among your descendants!* And I will continue this agreement between us generation after generation, forever, for
it shall be between me and your children as well. It is a
contract that I shall be your God and the God of your
posterity. And I will give all this land of Canaan to you
and them, forever. And I will be your God' " (only the
material in brackets is mine).

Then God reassured Abraham (his new name) that Sarai
would bear him the promised seed of many nations.

It's interesting to note here that Ishmael was born to
Abram *before* the covenant was sealed. The sealing of that
covenant was marked by the changing of Abram's name
(which translates "Exalted Father") to Abraham (which
translates "Father of Nations").

OT *Genesis 17:15-21:* "Then God added, 'Regarding Sarai your
wife—her name is no longer "Sarai" but "Sarah" ("Princess"). And I will bless her and give you a son from her!
Yes, I will bless her richly, and make her the mother of
nations! Many kings shall be among your posterity.' Then
Abraham threw himself down in worship before the Lord,
but inside he was laughing in disbelief! 'Me, be a father?'
he said in amusement. 'Me—100 years old? And Sarah, to
have a baby at 90?' And Abraham said to God, 'Yes, do
bless Ishmael!' [This statement was really saying to God,
'Are you *sure* it's Sarah who will give me the seed of
many nations? Do you mean Ishmael?'] 'No,' God replied,
'that isn't what I said. [Patience—what patience God has
with his children. He permitted Abraham to ask for confirmation, just as he does the believer of today.] *Sarah* shall
bear you a son; and you are to name him Isaac ("Laughter"), and I will sign my covenant with him forever, and

with *his* descendants. As for Ishmael, all right, I will bless him also, just as you have asked me to. I will cause him to multiply and become a great nation. Twelve princes shall be among his posterity. But my contract is with Isaac, who will be born to you and Sarah next year at about this time.' " [Covenant confirmed!]

First, let's take a look at Sarah's name-change. She went from Sarai (translates "dominative") to Sarah (translates "princess"). A princess is authoritatively under a king. Sarah went from dominating her husband to submitting to her King—God Almighty. She would ultimately understand and *believe*, but these things take time. We are not changed from black to white overnight; God does not work that way!

Second, let's take a look at God's incredible sense of humor! Did you notice the name he chose for Abraham's seed . . . the seed of many nations? Isaac, which translates "laughter." It was their laughter which characterized the concern of Abraham and Sarah that God could fulfill his promise in their aged bodies. But it was also to be laughter which characterized their joy when Isaac was born. This is strictly my own opinion, but I believe it is also laughter which characterizes God's joy of fulfilling the promises he makes to his children, much to our amazement!

OT *Genesis 18:12–14:* "So Sarah laughed silently. 'A woman my age have a baby?' she scoffed to herself. 'And with a husband as old as mine?' Then God said to Abraham, 'Why did Sarah laugh? Why did she say "Can an old woman like me have a baby?" *Is anything too hard for God?* Next year, just as I told you, I will certainly see to it that Sarah has a son.' "

No . . . *nothing* is too hard for God!

Matthew 19:26: "But Jesus beheld them, and said unto them, With men this is impossible, but *with God all things are possible*" (KJV).

OT *Psalm 37:5:* "Commit thy way unto the Lord; trust also in him, and *he shall bring it to pass*" (KJV).

And so, the promise was fulfilled in the birth of Isaac.

OT *Genesis 21:1–7:* "Then God did as he had promised, and Sarah became pregnant and gave Abraham a baby son in his old age, *at the time God had said;* and Abraham named him Isaac (meaning 'Laughter'). Eight days after he was born, Abraham circumcised him, as God required. (Abraham was 100 years old at that time.) And Sarah declared, 'God has brought me laughter! All who hear about this shall rejoice with me. For who would have dreamed that I would ever have a baby? Yet I have given Abraham a child in his old age!' " (Parentheses not mine.)

Here the key words for believers are "at the time God said"; according to *his* plans, not ours. We can see that through the trials of Abraham and Sarah God taught them that he is faithful to his promises and they learned another invaluable lesson—patience. It is a lesson he is intent on teaching all his children. Why? Because patience is such a blessing.

Romans 5:3–5: "We can rejoice, too, when we run into problems and trials for we know that they are good for us —they help us learn to be patient. And patience develops strength of character in us and helps us trust God more each time we use it until finally our hope and faith are strong and steady. Then, when that happens, we are able to hold our heads high no matter what happens and know that all is well, for we know how dearly God loves us, and we feel this warm love everywhere within us because God has given us the Holy Spirit to fill our hearts with his love."

We learn to trust God no matter what our circumstances.

ot   *Jeremiah 29:11:* "For I know the plans I have for you, says the Lord. They are plans for good and not for evil, to give you a future and a hope."

(Isn't God neat? And isn't the Old Testament rich?)

Yes, Sarah gave Abraham a child in his old age, but not just any child! In Isaac God began to fulfill his promise to Abraham that he would be the father of many nations, and the Jewish nation began with Isaac. But, more importantly, Jesus Christ would come forth from the seed of Isaac!

It's also interesting to note that God promised that Ishmael would become the father of a mighty nation too, and that nation today is the Arab world! (As an aside, it is fascinating to note that all eyes today are focused on the Middle East, where the Arabs and the Jews are in great conflict! And it all began with Abraham!)

Because Ishmael was born out of sin and disobedience (to God) with Hagar, an Egyptian, Egypt symbolizes "evil and wickedness" in the Bible. This does not mean that God loves Egypt or the Arabs any less than he loves the rest of the world, for we are *all* his creatures, Jew and Gentile alike. (All who are not Jews are Gentiles according to the Bible. But of course not all Gentiles are Christians.) Nor does it mean the Arabs are more evil and wicked than the rest of us. It is merely a *symbol.* (It will be important in our study "Types and Shadows of Christ in the Old Testament" to know this symbolism. That is why I mention it here.)

Now that we know how the Jews were chosen, let's examine why they were chosen.

The Jews were chosen to be an example to the world—a light that all could see—for loving and serving God.

OT *Isaiah 42:6–7:* "I the Lord have called you to demonstrate my righteousness. I will guard and support you, for I have given you to my people as the personal confirmation of my covenant with them. *You shall also be a light to guide the nations [the Gentiles] unto me. You will open the eyes of the blind, and release those who sit in prison darkness and despair.*"

This Scripture specifically refers to the Messiah, but in general to the "chosen" ones of Israel. Their purpose: to be a "light to guide the nations to God . . . to open the eyes of the blind . . . to release the imprisoned from the darkness and despair of disbelief."

OT *Isaiah 62:2:* "The nations [the Gentiles] shall see your [Israel's] righteousness. Kings shall be blinded by your glory; and God will confer on you a new name."

But one of the most beautiful Scriptures of prophecy about this is . . .

OT *Isaiah 49:1–7, 14:* "Listen to me, all of you in far-off lands: The Lord called me [the Messiah] before my birth. From within the womb he called me by my name. God will make my words of judgment sharp as swords. He has hidden me in the shadow of His hand; I am like a sharp arrow in His quiver.

"He said to me: 'You are my Servant, a Prince of Power with God, and you shall bring me glory.'

"I replied, 'But my work for them seems all in vain; I have spent my strength for them without response. Yet I leave it all with God for my reward.'

" 'And now,' said the Lord—the Lord who formed me from my mother's womb to serve him who commissioned me to restore to him his people Israel, who has given me the strength to perform this task and honored me for doing it!—'you shall do more than restore Israel to me. *I will make you a Light to the nations of the world to bring my salvation to them too.'*

"The Lord, the Redeemer and Holy One of Israel, says to the one who is despised, rejected by mankind, and kept beneath the heel of earthly rulers [the Messiah]: 'Kings shall stand at attention when you pass by; princes shall bow low because the Lord has chosen you; he, the faithful Lord, the Holy One of Israel, chooses you. . . . Yet they say, 'My Lord deserted us; he has forgotten us [the Jews].' ' "

Here is a beautiful "picture" of the Messiah to come . . . and yet the Jews have not accepted him. Why?

There is a great deal of prophecy regarding this subject. Ten times in the Old Testament God refers to his chosen ones as a "stiff-necked people."

OT   *Exodus 33:3:* "Unto a land flowing with milk and honey: for I will not go up in the midst of thee; for thou art a stiffnecked people: lest I consume thee in the way" (KJV). (See also Exod. 32:9; 33:5; 34:9; Deut. 9:6; 9:13; 10:16; Psa. 75:5; Jer. 17:23; Ezek. 2:4; and Acts 7:51.)

Why did the Lord call his beloved chosen ones "stiff-necked?" Because they were continually disobedient and failed to understand God's love and desire for them.

OT   *Deuteronomy 10:15–16:* "Only the Lord had a delight in thy fathers [Israelites] to love them, and he chose their seed after them, even you above all people, as it is this day. *Circumcise therefore the foreskin of your heart,* and be no more stiffnecked" (KJV).

Romans 2:28–29: "For you are not real Jews just because you were born of Jewish parents or because you have gone

through the Jewish initiation ceremony of circumcision.
No, a real Jew is anyone whose heart is right with God.
For God is not looking for those who cut their bodies
in actual body circumcision, but he is looking for those
with changed hearts and minds. Whoever has that kind
of change in his life will get the praise from God, even if
not from you."

Romans 2:28–29: "For he is not a Jew, which is one out-
wardly; neither is that circumcision, which is outward
in the flesh: But he is a Jew, which is one inwardly; and
circumcision is that of the heart, in the spirit, and not in
the letter [of the law]; whose praise is not of men, but
of God" (KJV).

Because of the continued disobedience and rebellion of his
chosen people, the Lord became angry toward them—

OT **Jeremiah 6:18–21:** "Therefore hear, ye nations, and know,
O congregation what is among them. Hear, O earth:
behold, I will bring evil upon this people, even the fruit
of their thoughts, because they have not hearkened unto
my words, nor to my law, but rejected it. To what purpose cometh there to me incense from Sheba, and the
sweet cane from a far country? Your burnt offerings are
not acceptable, nor your sacrifices sweet unto me. Therefore thus saith the Lord, Behold, I will lay stumblingblocks before this people, and the fathers and the sons
together shall fall upon them; the neighbour and his
friend shall perish" (KJV).

OT **Jeremiah 7:21–28:** "The Lord of Hosts, the God of Israel
says, Away with your offerings and sacrifices! It wasn't
offerings and sacrifices I wanted from your fathers when
I led them out of Egypt. That was not the point of my
command. But what I told them was: *Obey me* and I will
be your God and you shall be my people; only do as I
say and all shall be well! But they wouldn't listen; they
kept on doing whatever they wanted to, following their
own stubborn, evil thoughts. They went backward instead
of forward. Ever since the day your fathers left Egypt
until now, I have kept on sending them my prophets,
day after day. But they wouldn't listen to them or even
try to hear. They are hard and stubborn and rebellious—

worse even than their fathers were. Tell them everything that I will do to them, but don't expect them to listen. Cry out your warnings, but don't expect them to respond. Say to them: This is the nation that refuses to obey the Lord its God, and refuses to be taught. She continues to live a lie."

The result of God's anger toward his chosen people lies in . . .

OT *Jeremiah 6:21:* "Therefore, thus saith the Lord, *Behold, I will lay stumblingblocks before this people,* and the fathers and the sons together shall fall upon them; the neighbour and his friend shall perish" (KJV).

What were those stumblingblocks?

Romans 9:31–32: "But the Jews, who tried so hard to get right with God by keeping his laws, never succeeded. Why not? Because they were trying to be saved by keeping the law and being good instead of by depending on faith. *They have stumbled over the great stumbling stone.*"

Romans 10:1–4: "Dear brothers, the longing of my heart and my prayer is that the Jewish people might be saved. I know what enthusiasm they have for the honor of God, but it is misdirected zeal. For they don't understand that Christ has died to make them right with God. Instead they are trying to make themselves good enough to gain God's favor by keeping the Jewish laws and customs, but that is not God's way of salvation."

OT *Psalm 40:5–8:* "O Lord my God, many and many a time you have done great miracles for us, and we are ever in your thoughts. Who else can do such glorious things? No one else can be compared with you. There isn't time to tell of all your wonderful deeds. It isn't sacrifices and offerings which you really want from your people. Burnt animals bring no special joy to your heart. But you have accepted the offer of my lifelong service. Then I said, 'See, I have come, just as all the prophets foretold. And I delight to do your will, my God, for your law is written upon my heart!'"

God knew no one could ever keep his laws perfectly . . . not even the great men of the Bible succeeded in doing that

   . . . not Moses, not Abraham, not David . . . no, not one.

OT   *Psalm 14:2–3:* "The Lord looks down from heaven *on all mankind* to see if there are any who are wise, who want to please God. But no, all have strayed away; all are rotten with sin. Not one is good, not one!"

"Well," you might be thinking, "if God loved these people so much, why did he give them laws they could not keep perfectly?" The Law was given to them to prepare them for the Messiah—the Savior who would save them from their sin and self-righteousness—to show them just how much they really needed a Messiah.

   Romans 3:20: "Now do you see it? No one can ever be made right in God's sight by doing what the law commands. For the more we know of God's laws, the clearer it becomes that we aren't obeying them; his laws serve only to make us see that we are sinners."

   Romans 7:7: "Well then, am I suggesting that these laws of God are evil? Of course not! No, the law is not sinful but it was the law that showed me my sin. I would never have known the sin in my heart—the evil desires that are hidden there—if the law had not said, 'You must not have evil desires in your heart.' "

OT   *Psalm 143:2:* "And enter not into judgment with thy servant: *for in thy sight shall no man living be justified*" (KJV).

But God did promise that there would be time in the future when the Mosaic Covenant—the Law—would no longer be the standard for righteousness.

THE OLD TESTAMENT:

OT   *Isaiah 43:18–19:* "Remember ye not the former things, neither consider the things of old. Behold, I will do a new thing; now it shall spring forth; shall ye not know it? I will even make a way in the wilderness, and rivers in the desert" (KJV).

OT   *Jeremiah 31:31–34:* "Behold, the days come, saith the Lord, that I will make a new covenant with the house of Israel, and with the house of Judah: *Not according to the covenant that I made with their fathers in the day that I took them by the hand to bring them out of the land of Egypt;*

which my covenant they **brake** [*the Mosaic Covenant—
the Law*], although I was an husband unto them, saith
the Lord: But this shall be the covenant that I will make
with the house of Israel; After those days, saith the Lord,
*I will put my law in their inward parts, and write it in
their hearts;* and will be their God, and they shall be my
people. And they shall teach no more every man his
neighbour, and every man his brother, saying, Know the
Lord: for they shall all know me, from the least of them
unto the greatest of them, saith the Lord: for I will forgive their iniquity, and I will remember their sin no more"
(KJV).

NEW TESTAMENT:

Romans 10:4: "For Christ is the end of the law for righteousness to everyone that believeth" (KJV).
Romans 7:6: "But now we are delivered from the law, that
being dead wherein we were held; that we should *serve
in newness of spirit,* and not in the oldness of the letter"
(KJV).

Jesus Christ, the Messiah, died for the sins of the world, but,
in addition to the law, he too became a stumbling block to
the Jews. There was much prophecy about this.

NEW TESTAMENT:

Romans 9:33: "God warned them of this in the Scriptures
when he said, 'I have put a Rock in the path of the Jews,
and many will stumble over him (Jesus). Those who believe in him will never be disappointed.'"

OLD TESTAMENT:

OT *Isaiah 8:14–15:* "He will be your safety; but Israel and Judah
have refused his care and thereby stumbled against the
Rock of their salvation and lie fallen and crushed beneath it. . . ."

OT *Isaiah 28:16:* "But the Lord God says, See, I am placing a
Foundation Stone in Zion—a firm, tested, precious Corner-
stone that is safe to build on. He who believes need never
run away again."

OT *Psalm 118:22:* "The stone rejected by the builders has now
become the capstone of the arch!" [literally, "the head of
the corner"]. (Brackets not mine.)

It all seems so clear to believers, but the Scriptures reveal
that there is a "veil" over the eyes of the Jews, that they
cannot see the truth.

NEW TESTAMENT:

2 Corinthians 3:14–15: "Not only Moses' face was veiled, but
his people's minds and understanding were veiled and
blinded too. Even now when the Scripture is read it seems
as though Jewish hearts and minds are covered by a thick
veil, because they cannot see and understand the real
meaning of the Scriptures. For this veil of misunderstand-
ing can be removed only by believing in Christ. Yes, even
today when they read Moses' writings their hearts are
blind and they think that obeying the Ten Commandments is the way to be saved."

OLD TESTAMENT:

OT *Deuteronomy 29:3–4:* "You have seen with your own eyes
the great plagues and mighty miracles that the Lord
brought upon Pharaoh and his people in the land of
Egypt. But even yet the Lord hasn't given you hearts
that understand or eyes that see or ears that hear!"

OT *Isaiah 6:9–10:* "And he said, 'Yes, go. But tell my people this:
"Though you hear my words repeatedly, you won't understand them. Though you watch and watch as I perform
my miracles, still you won't know what they mean."'"

OT *Isaiah 29:10:* "For the Lord has poured out upon you a spirit
of deep sleep. He has closed the eyes of your prophets
and seers."

But God's plan for his children is perfect. He has not forsaken his chosen people; he has a plan for waking them from their "sleep."

NEW TESTAMENT:

Romans 10:19: "And did they understand [that God would give his salvation to others if they refused to take it]? (these brackets not mine). Yes, for even back in the time of Moses, God had said that he would make his people jealous and try to wake them up by giving his salvation to the foolish heathen nations [the Gentiles]."

Romans 11:11: "Does this mean that God has rejected his Jewish people forever? Of course not! His purpose was to make his salvation available to the Gentiles, and then the Jews would be jealous and begin to want God's salvation for themselves."

OLD TESTAMENT:

OT *Deuteronomy 32:21:* "They have made me very jealous of their idols, which are not gods at all. Now I, in turn, will make them jealous by giving my affections to the foolish Gentile nations of the world."

NEW TESTAMENT:

Romans 9:25: "Remember what the prophecy of Hosea says? There God says that he will find other children for Himself (who are not from his Jewish family) and will love them, though no one had ever loved them before."

OLD TESTAMENT:

OT *Hosea 2:23:* "At that time I will sow a crop of Israelites and raise them for myself! I will pity those who are 'not pitied,' and I will say to those who are 'not my people,' 'Now you are my people'; and they will reply, 'You are our God!' "

NEW TESTAMENT:

Romans 9:26: "And the heathen, of whom it once was said, 'You are not my people,' shall be called 'sons of the Living God.'"

OLD TESTAMENT:

OT **Hosea 1:10:** " 'Yet the time will come when Israel shall prosper and become a great nation; in that day her people will be too numerous to count—like sand along a seashore! Then, instead of saying to them, "You are not my people," I will tell them, "You are my sons, children of the Living God." ' "

Remember in the "Definitions" chapter I mentioned that Christians are "adopted Jews" and are therefore considered a part of Israel too? The above Scripture is the Old Testament authority for this. The Gentile Christians are the "ones who were not his people, but are now his sons, children of the Living God."

NEW TESTAMENT:

Romans 10:20: "And later on Isaiah said boldly that God would be found by people who weren't even looking for him."

OLD TESTAMENT:

OT **Isaiah 65:1:** "The Lord says, People who never before inquired about me are now seeking me out. Nations who never before searched for me are finding me."

NEW TESTAMENT:

Romans 10:21: "In the meantime, he keeps on reaching out his hands to the Jews, but they keep arguing and refusing to come."

OLD TESTAMENT:

OT *Isaiah 65:2:* "But my own people—though I have been
    spreading out my arms to welcome them [the Jews] all
    day long—have rebelled; they follow their own evil paths
    and thoughts."

We can clearly see from the previous Scriptures that the
Gentiles were very much a part of God's plan to make the
Jews jealous and draw them back into his breast. By accept-
ing Jesus Christ as our Lord and Savior (Messiah), we are
adopted into the family of God. We are Jews by adoption!
Romans 2:28–29: "For you are not real Jews just because
    you were born of Jewish parents or because you have gone
    through the Jewish initiation ceremony of circumcision.
    No, *a real Jew is anyone whose heart is right with God.*
    For God is not looking for those who cut their bodies in
    actual body circumcision, but he is looking for those with
    changed hearts and minds. *Whoever has that kind of
    change in his life will get his praise from God, even if
    not from you."* (Romans was written by Paul—a com-
    pleted Jew.)
Here we have a beautiful "picture" of Ezekiel 36:26: "And
I will give you a new heart—I will give you new and right
desires—and put a new spirit within you. *I will take out
your stony hearts of sin and give you new hearts of love."*
    This verse perfectly illustrates the circumcision of the
heart—the changed life.
Romans 11:17: "But some of these branches from Abraham's
    tree, some of the Jews, have been broken off. And *you
    Gentiles who were branches from, we might say, a wild
    olive tree, were grafted in. So now you, too, receive the
    blessing God has promised Abraham and his children,
    sharing in God's rich nourishment of his own special olive
    tree."* [The roots of this tree are Jesus Christ; we are his
    branches.]
Romans 11:17 fulfills . . .
OT *Genesis 12:3:* "I will bless those who bless you [Abraham]
    and curse those who curse you; and *the entire world will
    be blessed because of you."*

The above verse says it all. The Jews are very special people to Christians. We are blessed through the Jews by Jesus Christ . . . and because New Testament faith and Old Testament faith are the same. As Edith Schaeffer says, *Christianity is Jewish!*

Romans 4:16–25: "So God's blessings are given to us by faith, as a free gift; we are certain to get them whether or not we follow Jewish customs if we have faith like Abraham's, for Abraham is the father of us all when it comes to these matters of faith. That is what the Scriptures mean when they say that God made Abraham the father of many nations. God will accept all people in every nation who trust God as Abraham did. And this promise is from God himself, who makes the dead live again and speaks of future events with as much certainty as though they were already past.

"So, when God told Abraham that he would give him a son who would have many descendants and become a great nation, Abraham believed God even though such a promise just couldn't come to pass! And because his faith was strong, he didn't worry about the fact that he was too old to be a father, at the age of one hundred, and that Sarah his wife, at ninety, was also much too old to have a baby.

"But Abraham never doubted. He believed God, for his faith and trust grew ever stronger, and he praised God for this blessing even before it happened. He was completely sure that God was well able to do anything he promised. And because of Abraham's faith God forgave his sins and declared him 'not guilty.'

"Now this wonderful statement—that he was accepted and approved through his faith—wasn't just for Abraham's benefit. It was for us, too, assuring us that God will accept us in the same way he accepted Abraham—when we believe the promises of God who brought back Jesus our Lord from the dead. He died for our sins and rose again to make us right with God, filling us with God's goodness."

It is *faith* that saves man, from Genesis to Revelation.

Ephesians 2:8–9: "For by grace are ye saved *through faith* [trust; believing]; and that not of yourselves: it is the gift of God: Not of works, lest any man should boast" (KJV).

OT   **Joel 2:32:** "Everyone who calls upon the name of the Lord will be saved. . . .'"

OT   **Genesis 15:6:** "And he [Abraham] believed in the Lord; and he [God] counted it to him [Abraham] for righteousness" (KJV).

OT   **Micah 6:6–8:** " 'How can we make up to you for what we've done?' you ask. 'Shall we bow before the Lord with offerings of yearling calves?' Oh, no! For if you offered him thousands of rams and ten thousands of rivers of olive oil—would that please him? Would he be satisfied? If you sacrificed your oldest child, would that make him glad? Then would he forgive your sins? Of course not! No, he has told you what he wants, and this is all it is: to be fair and just and merciful, and to walk humbly with your God."

OT   **Jeremiah 17:7:** "But blessed is the man who trusts in the Lord and has made the Lord his hope and confidence."

OT   **Habakkuk 2:4:** "Note this: Wicked men trust themselves alone, and fail; but the righteous man trusts in me, and lives!"

     Romans 5:1: "Therefore being justified by faith, we have peace with God through our Lord Jesus Christ" (KJV).

     Acts 2:21: "And it shall come to pass, that whosoever shall call on the name of the Lord shall be saved" (KJV).

     Romans 10:13: "Anyone who calls upon the name of the Lord will be saved."

We have learned in this chapter that the Jews *are* God's chosen ones. And, as Christians, we should never lose sight of this fact, because *they still are his chosen ones!*

OT   **Isaiah 54:5–10:** "For your Creator will be your 'husband.' The Lord of Hosts is his name; he is your Redeemer, the Holy One of Israel, the God of all the earth. For the Lord has called you back from your grief—a young wife abandoned by her husband. For a brief moment I abandoned you. But with great compassion I will gather you. In a moment of anger I turned my face a little while; but with everlasting love I will have pity on you, says the Lord, your Redeemer. Just as in the time of Noah I swore that I would never again permit the waters of a flood to cover the earth and destroy its life, so now I swear that I will never again pour out my anger on you as I have during this exile. For the mountains may depart and the hills disappear, but my kindness shall not leave you. My promise of peace for you will never be broken, says the Lord who has mercy upon you."

OT   *Ezekiel 39:21–29:* "Thus I will demonstrate my glory among the nations [the Gentiles]; all shall see the punishment of God and know that I have done it. 'And from that time onward, the people of Israel will know I am the Lord their God. And the nations will know why Israel was sent away to exile—it was punishment for sin, for they acted in treachery against their God. Therefore I turned my face away from them and let their enemies destroy them. I turned my face away and punished them in proportion to the vileness of their sins. But now, the Lord God says, I will end the captivity of my people and have mercy upon them and restore their fortunes, for I am concerned about my reputation! Their time of treachery and shame will all be in the past; they will be home again, in peace and safety in their own land, with no one bothering them or making them afraid. I will bring them home from the lands of their enemies—and my glory shall be evident to all the nations when I do it. Through them I will vindicate my holiness before the nations. Then my people will know I am the Lord their God—responsible for sending them away to exile, and responsible for bringing them home. I will leave none of them remaining among the nations. And I will never hide my face from them again, for I will pour out my Spirit upon them, says the Lord God.' "

How much the Lord God Almighty loves his chosen ones!

Romans 11:24–32: "For if God was willing to take you who were so far away from him—being part of a wild olive tree—and graft you into his own good tree—a very unusual thing to do—don't you see that he will be far more ready to put the Jews back again, who were there in the first place?

"I want you to know about this truth from God, dear

brothers, so that you will not feel proud and start brag-
ging. Yes, it is true that some of the Jews have set themselves against the Gospel now, but this will last only
until all of you Gentiles have come to Christ—those of you
who will. And then all Israel will be saved. Do you remember what the prophets said about this? 'There shall
come out of Zion a Deliverer [Jesus Christ], and he shall
turn the Jews from all ungodliness. At that time I will
take away their sins, just as I promised.'

"Now many of the Jews are enemies of the Gospel.
They hate it. But this has been a benefit to you, for it has
resulted in God's giving his gifts to you Gentiles. Yet
*the Jews are still beloved of God because of his promises
to Abraham, Isaac, and Jacob. For God's gifts and his
call can never be withdrawn; he will never go back on his
promises.* Once you were rebels against God, but when
the Jews refused his gifts God was merciful to you instead. *And now the Jews are the rebels, but some day they
too will share in God's mercy upon you.* For God has given
them all up to sin so that he could have mercy upon all
alike."

We owe a great debt to the Jews . . . for the centuries of
sparing not their own lives to preserve God's Word for themselves and the nations of the world . . . for being a light
to us . . . for Jesus Christ, the seed of Abraham, our
Redeemer. The payment for that debt is compassion for
God's Chosen Ones—and our deepest love and affection.

Pray for the Jewish people . . .

Romans 10:1: "Dear brothers, the longing of my heart and
my prayers is that the Jewish people might be saved."

Paul's prayer for the Jews says it most poignantly . . .

Romans 9:1–5: "Oh, Israel, my people! Oh, my Jewish
brothers! How I long for you to come to Christ. My heart
is heavy within me and I grieve bitterly day and night because of you. Christ knows and the Holy Spirit knows
that it is no mere pretense when I say that I would be
willing to be forever damned if that would save you.
God has given you so much, but still you will not listen
to him. He took you as his own special, chosen people
and led you along with a bright cloud of glory and told

you how very much he wanted to bless you. He gave you his rules for daily life so you would know what he wanted you to do. He let you worship him, and gave you mighty promises. Great men of God were your fathers, and Christ himself was one of you, a Jew so far as his human nature is concerned, he who now rules over all things. Praise God forever!"

Pray for peace in Israel . . .

OT   *Psalm 122:6:* "Pray for the peace of Jerusalem. May all who love this city prosper."

What a merciful and mighty God we have!

OT   *Zephaniah 3:17:* "The Lord thy God in the midst of thee is mighty; he will save, he will rejoice over thee with joy; he will rest in his love, he will joy over thee with singing" (KJV).

Most important of all, let's not be a stumbling block to the Jews. For almost two thousand years they have been persecuted in the name of Jesus by pseudo-Christians (e.g., Nazis who called themselves Christians) and untaught Christians. Recognize how important they are to God's plan and what an error this persecution is and has been. Love them for who they are—God's chosen people.

An Important Name—Jesus Christ

SINCE NAMES ARE so important to the Lord (as we saw in the previous chapter), it seems fitting to examine Jesus' names. Although Jesus' name does not actually appear in the Old Testament, a look at word relationships between Old and New Testaments is helpful. The *Yeshua Hamashiach* of the New Testament is a coupling of one Hebrew form for Jesus (*Yeshua*) with the Hebrew *Mashiach,* meaning "Messiah" or "Anointed One." (The letters *Ha* preceding the root word correspond to the definite article *the.*) Another Hebrew form for Jesus is *Jehoshua,* literally, "Jehovah saves." *Jehovah,* in turn, is the transliteration for the Hebrew Tetragrammaton JHWH, or God, and also means self-existent or eternal. The name *Jesus* can thus very literally be translated "Jehovah (or God) saves."

In the New Testament, the name *Christ* is translated from the Greek *Christos,* literally, "Anointed," or "Messiah." The Greek word for Jesus, *Iesous,* is the Hebrew "Jehoshua," or, as above, "God saves."

Another very interesting thing on this subject involves one of the Christian symbols, the fish ⌀. In the early times of Christianity, when it was not "safe" openly to declare one's belief in Jesus Christ the Messiah, the fish was a code. As a believer approached a person or persons about whom he was unsure, he would draw an arc in the dirt with his shoe, ⌒, one-half of a fish. If the other person was a believer, he would complete the fish with the second arc, ⌣. Thus we have ⌀.

The significance of this Christian symbol is that the Greek

word for fish is *ichthus,* an acronym in which the letters stand for the initial letters of "Jesus Christ God's Son, Savior," or *I*esous *Ch*ristos *Th*eou *U*ios Sōtēr.

It's fascinating to me that there is never any waste in God's "economy" of things. Even the names are important!

Prophecy in the Old Testament

THERE ARE 333 prophecies in the Old Testament regarding the first coming of Jesus Christ, the Messiah. Every one of those 333 prophecies was fulfilled in the New Testament.

Some computer scientists at the University of Oregon ran this through a computer to ascertain the odds of one man's fulfilling 333 prophecies. They found that the odds against it were 67^{10} or 670,000,000,000*—not exactly infinity, but greater than our national debt! This should be enough to stimulate even the greatest minds!

In this short book, there's no way to give every example of prophecy and fulfillment in the Bible, but we can share a few. Seeing the importance and relevance of the Old Testament to the New can give you a love and appreciation for it that you never had before.

THE PROPHECY:

OT *Genesis 3:15:* "And I will put enmity between thee [the serpent, who was Satan] and the woman, and between thy seed and *her seed; it [the Messiah] shall bruise thy head, and thou shalt bruise his heel"* (KJV).

Here in Genesis is the first prophecy of the Messiah, who would (1) be born of the seed of woman (not man); and (2) would defeat Satan and sin and death. It is important to mention that nowhere else in the Old Testament does it *ever* refer to the "seed of woman" except in Isaiah 7:14, which is also a prophecy of the birth of the Messiah.

* *Michael, Michael, Why Do You Hate Me?* by Michael Esses. Copyright © 1973 by Logos International. All rights reserved. Used by permission.

226

OT **Isaiah 7:14:** "Therefore the Lord Himself shall give you a
sign, Behold, the young woman who is unmarried and a
virgin shall conceive and bear a son, and shall call his
name Immanuel—God with us" (*Amplified Bible*).
Everywhere else that reference is made to human "seed"
it is to the "seed of man."

THE FULFILLMENT (1)

Luke 1:28–35: "And the angel came in unto her, and said,
Hail, thou art highly favoured, the Lord is with thee:
blessed art thou among women. And when she saw him,
she was troubled at his saying, and cast in her mind what
manner of salutation this should be. And the angel said
unto her, Fear not, Mary: for thou hast found favour with
God. And, behold, thou shalt conceive in thy womb, and
bring forth a son, and shalt call his name JESUS. He shall
be great, and shall be called the Son of the Highest: and
the Lord God shall give unto him the throne of his father
David: and he shall reign over the house of Jacob for
ever; and of his kingdom there shall be no end. Then
said Mary unto the angel, How shall this be, seeing *I
know not a man?* [I am a virgin.] And the angel answered
and said unto her, The Holy Ghost shall come upon thee,
and the power of the Highest shall overshadow thee:
therefore also that holy thing which shall be born of
thee shall be called the Son of God" (KJV).

Matthew 1:22–23: "Now all this was done, that it might be
fulfilled which was spoken of the Lord by the prophet,
saying, Behold, a virgin shall be with child, and shall
bring forth a son, and they shall call his name Emmanuel,
which being interpreted is, God with us" (KJV).
The second prophecy in Genesis 3:15 foretells of the defeat
of sin and death by the "bruising of Satan's head.". . .

THE FULFILLMENT (2)

Colossians 2:13–15: "You were dead [spiritually] in sins,
and your sinful desires were not yet cut away. Then he
gave you a share in the very life of Christ, for he forgave
all your sins, and blotted out the charges proved against

you, the list of his commandments which you had not obeyed. He took this list of sins and destroyed it by nailing it to Christ's cross. In this way God took away Satan's power to accuse you of sin, and God openly displayed to the whole world Christ's triumph at the cross where your sins were taken away."

Hebrews 2:14: "Since we, God's children, are human beings —made of flesh and blood—he became flesh and blood too by being born in human form; for only as a human being could he die and in dying break the power of the devil who had the power of death."

Yet Christ's agonizing death on the cross was no more than a "bruise to his heel.". . . He is alive.

THE FULFILLMENT (3)

1 Corinthians 15:3–6, 20: "I passed on to you right from the first what had been told to me (firsthand), that Christ died for our sins just as the Scriptures said he would, and that he was buried, and that three days afterwards he arose from the grave just as the prophets foretold. He was seen by Peter and later by the rest of 'the Twelve.' After that he was seen by more than five hundred Christian brothers at one time, most of whom are still alive, though some have died by now. But the fact is that Christ did actually rise from the dead. . . ."

1 Corinthians 15:55–57: "O death, where then your victory? Where then your sting? For sin—the sting that causes death—will all be gone; and the law, which reveals our sins, will no longer be our judge. How we thank God for all of this! It is he who makes us victorious through Jesus Christ our Lord!"

THE PROPHECY:

OT   *Isaiah 53:1–11:* "But, oh, how few believe it: Who will listen? To whom will God reveal his saving power? In God's eyes he was like a tender green shoot, sprouting from a root in dry and sterile ground. But in our eyes there was no attractiveness at all, nothing to make us want him. We despised him and rejected him—a man of sorrows, acquainted with bitterest grief. We turned our backs on him and looked the other way when he went by. He was despised and we didn't care.

"Yet it was *our* grief he bore, *our* sorrows that weighed him down. And we thought his troubles were a punishment from God, for his *own* sins! But he was wounded and bruised for *our* sins. He was chastised that we might have peace; he was lashed—and we were healed! *We* are the ones who strayed away like sheep! *We*, who left God's paths to follow our own. Yet God laid on *him* the guilt and sins of every one of us!

"He was oppressed and he was afflicted, yet he never said a word. He was brought as a lamb to the slaughter; and as a sheep before her shearers is dumb, so he stood silent before the ones condemning him. From prison and trial they led him away to his death. But who among the people of that day realized it was their sins that he was dying for—that he was suffering their punishment? He was buried like a criminal in a rich man's grave; but he had done no wrong, and had never spoken an evil word.

"Yet it was the Lord's good plan to bruise him and fill him with grief. But when his soul has been made an offering for sin, then he shall have a multitude of children, many heirs. He shall live again and God's program shall prosper in his hands. And when he sees all that is accomplished by the anguish of his soul, he shall be satisfied; and because of what he has experienced, my righteous Servant shall make many to be counted righteous before God, for he shall bear all their sins."

For detail, let's go over that last prophecy verse by verse.

OT **v. 1:** "But, oh, how few believe it: Who will listen? To whom will God reveal his saving power?"

THE FULFILLMENT:

Romans 10:16: "But *not everyone who hears the Good News has welcomed it,* for Isaiah the prophet said, "Lord, who has believed me when I told them?"

Acts 17:32: "And when they heard of the resurrection of the dead, *some mocked;* and others said, We will hear thee again of this matter" (KJV).

OT   *vv. 3–6:* "We despised him and rejected him—a man of sorrows, acquainted with bitterest grief. We turned our backs on him and looked the other way when he went by. He was despised and we didn't care. Yet it was *our* grief he bore, *our* sorrows that weighed him down. And we thought his troubles were a punishment from God, for his *own* sins! But he was wounded and bruised for our sins. He was chastised that we might have peace; he was lashed—and we were healed! *We* are the ones who strayed away like sheep! *We,* who left God's paths to follow our own. Yet God laid on *him* the guilt and sins of every one of us!"

THE FULFILLMENT:

1 Peter 2:22: "*He never sinned,* never told a lie." [He therefore *did not die for his sins, but for ours.*]

Matthew 27:26: "Then Pilate released Barabbas to them. And after *he had whipped Jesus,* he gave him to the Roman soldiers to take away and crucify." [He was lashed.]

1 Peter 2:24: "*He personally carried the load of our sins in his own body when he died on the cross,* so that we ca.. be finished with sin and live a good life from now on. For *his wounds have healed ours! Like sheep you wandered away from God,* but now you have returned to your Shepherd, the Guardian of your souls who keeps you safe from all attacks." [He was "wounded and bruised for our sins" and "we were healed." Yet "God laid on him the guilt and sins of every one of us!"]

Acts 26:22–23: "But God protected me so that I am still alive today to tell these facts to everyone, both great and small. I teach nothing except what the prophets and Moses said—that *the Messiah would suffer, and be the First to rise from the dead, to bring light to Jews and Gentiles alike.*"

OT   *v. 7:* "He was oppressed and he was afflicted, yet he never said a word. He was brought as a lamb to the slaughter; and as a sheep before her shearers is dumb, so he stood silent before the ones condemning him."

THE FULFILLMENT:

John 19:7–9: "They replied, 'By our laws he ought to die because he called himself the Son of God.' When Pilate
heard this, he was more frightened than ever. He took
Jesus back into the palace again and asked him, 'Where
are you from?' *but Jesus gave no answer.*" [He didn't defend himself.]

John 1:29: "The next day John saw Jesus coming toward
him and said, 'Look! There is *the Lamb of God* who takes
away the world's sin!" [The lamb led to slaughter.]

OT *v. 8:* "From prison and trial they led him away to his death.
But who among the people of that day realized it was
their sins that he was dying for—that he was suffering
their punishment?"

THE FULFILLMENT:

John 19:16–17: "Then Pilate gave Jesus to them to be crucified. So they had him at last, and *he was taken out of the
city,* carrying his cross to the place known as 'The Skull,'
in Hebrew, 'Golgotha.'" [They led him away to his death,
but how many of those people knew they were crucifying
the Messiah? Not one . . . or they would never have
done it!]

OT *v. 9:* "He was buried like a criminal in a rich man's grave;
but he had done no wrong, and had never spoken an evil
word."

THE FULFILLMENT:

Matthew 27:57–60: "When evening came, *a rich man* from
Arimathea named Joseph, one of Jesus' followers, went to
Pilate and asked for Jesus' body. And Pilate issued an
order to release it to him. *Joseph took the body and
wrapped it in a clean linen cloth, and placed it in his own
new rock-hewn tomb,* and rolled a great stone across the
entrance as he left." [Jesus was buried in a rich man's
grave.]

1 Peter 2:22: "He never sinned, never told a lie." [He was
without sin. He had done no wrong.]

OT   *v. 10:* "Yet it was the Lord's good plan to bruise him and fill him with grief. But when his soul has been made an offering for sin, then he shall have a multitude of children, many heirs. He shall live again and God's program shall prosper in his hands."

THE FULFILLMENT:

Romans 3:25: "For God sent Christ Jesus to take the punishment for our sins and to end all God's anger against us. He used Christ's blood and our faith as the means of saving us from his wrath. In this way he was being entirely fair, even though he did not punish those who sinned in former times [in the Old Testament]. For he was looking forward to the time when Christ would come and take away those sins." [He was an offering for the sins of the world.]

Matthew 28:6: "But he isn't here! For he has come back to life again, just as he said he would. Come in and see where his body was lying." [He "shall live again."]

OT   *v. 11:* "And when he sees all that is accomplished by the anguish of his soul, he shall be satisfied; and because of what he has experienced, my righteous Servant shall make many to be counted righteous before God, for he shall bear all their sins."

THE FULFILLMENT:

2 Corinthians 5:21: "For God took the sinless Christ and poured into him our sins. Then, in exchange, he poured God's goodness into us!"

1 Peter 2:24–25: "He personally carried the load of our sins in his own body when he died on the cross, so that we can be finished with sin and live a good life from now on. For his wounds have healed ours! Like sheep you wandered away from God, but now you have returned to your Shepherd, the Guardian of your souls who keeps you safe from all attacks."

THE PROPHECY:

OT   *Psalm 22:1:* "My God, my God, why have you forsaken me? Why do you refuse to help me or even to listen to my groans?"

THE FULFILLMENT:

Matthew 27:46: "About three o'clock, Jesus shouted, 'Eli, Eli, lama sabachthani,' which means, 'My God, my God, why have you forsaken me?'"

THE PROPHECY:

OT *Psalm 22:3–5:* "For you are holy. The praises of our fathers surrounded your throne; they trusted you and you delivered them. You heard their cries for help and saved them; they were never disappointed when they sought your aid."

THE FULFILLMENT:

2 Corinthians 5:21: "For God took the sinless Christ and poured into him our sins. Then, in exchange, he poured God's goodness into us!"

THE PROPHECY:

OT *Psalm 22:8:* " 'Is this the one who rolled his burdens on the Lord?' they laugh. 'Is this the one who claims the Lord delights in him? We'll believe it when we see God rescue him!' "

THE FULFILLMENT:

Luke 23:39: "One of the criminals hanging beside him scoffed, 'So you're the Messiah, are you? Prove it by saving yourself—and us, too, while you're at it!' "

THE PROPHECY:

OT *Psalm 22:14–18:* "My strength has drained away like water, and all my bones are out of joint. My heart melts like wax; my strength has dried up like sun-baked clay; my tongue sticks to my mouth, for you have laid me in the dust of death. The enemy, this gang of evil men, circles me like a pack of dogs; they have pierced my hands and feet. I can count every bone in my body. See these men of evil gloat and stare; they divide my clothes among themselves by a toss of the dice."

This entire body of Scripture is a picture of the crucifixion as it actually took place: the disjointed bones of his hands, wrists, arms, shoulders, and pelvis from hanging on the cross; perspiration caused by the intensity of the suffering pouring from the pores; the fluttering of the heart; the rapid physical debilitation and extreme dehydration; the nail-pierced hands and feet; the embarrassment and humiliation of nakedness exposed to jeering onwatchers—all associated with this type of death. It was a cruel and degrading way to die. In Matthew 27:35, the soldiers gambled at the foot of the cross for his robes. This particular prophecy is especially astonishing when you realize that crucifixion was not a Jewish form of execution, but rather a Roman one. Crucifixion had not even been thought of, much less performed, when this was written approximately one thousand years before the birth of Christ.

Another interesting fact about Christ's crucifixion is that it usually took a day or two to die this way—that's why it was such a cruel way to die. Crucifixion was a death of dehydration and shock. Yet Christ died within a matter of hours. He was God. *He died when he chose to die.*

Mark 15:37: "Then Jesus uttered another loud cry, and *dismissed his Spirit.*"

All 333 prophecies of the Messiah were fulfilled perfectly through Jesus Christ. Even his last words on the Cross, just before he died, were a fulfillment.

THE PROPHECY:

OT   *Psalm 69:21:* "For food they gave me poison; *for my awful thirst they offered me vinegar.*"

THE FULFILLMENT:

John 19:28–29: "Jesus knew that everything was now finished, and to fulfill the Scriptures said, 'I'm thirsty.' A jar of sour wine [which is vinegar] was sitting there, so a sponge was soaked in it and put on a hyssop branch and held up to his lips. When Jesus had tasted it, he said, 'It is finished,' and bowed his head and dismissed his spirit."

These prophecies all pointed to the Messiah, the Savior.
1 Peter 1:10–12: "This salvation was something the prophets

did not fully understand. Though they wrote about it, they had many questions as to what it all could mean. They wondered what the Spirit of Christ within them was talking about, for he told them to write down the events which, since then, have happened to Christ: his suffering, and his great glory afterwards. And they wondered when and to whom all this would happen.

"They were finally told that these things would not occur during their lifetime, but long years later, during yours. And now at last this Good News has been plainly announced to all of us. It was preached to us in the power of the same heaven-sent Holy Spirit who spoke to them; and it is all so strange and wonderful that even the angels in heaven would give a great deal to know more about it."

2 Peter 1:19–21: "So we have seen and proved that what the prophets said came true. You will do well to pay close attention to everything they have written, for, like lights shining into dark corners, their words help us to understand many things that otherwise would be dark and difficult. But when you consider the wonderful truth of the prophets' words, then the light will dawn in your souls and Christ the Morning Star will shine in your hearts. For no prophecy recorded in Scripture was ever thought up by the prophet himself. It was the Holy Spirit within these godly men who gave them true messages from God."

Was Jesus Christ the Son of God—God himself in the flesh?

THE PROPHECY:

OT *Psalm 40:7:* "Then I said, 'See, I have come, just as all the prophets foretold. I delight to do your will, my God, for your law is written upon my heart!' "

THE FULFILLMENT:

John 4:34: "Jesus saith unto them, My meat is to do the will of him that sent me, and to finish his work" (KJV).

John 1:45: "Philip now went off to look for Nathanael and told him, 'We have found the Messiah!—the very person Moses and the prophets told about! His name is Jesus, the son of Joseph from Nazareth!' "

Yes, Jesus Christ was the Son of God! Just examining a *few* of these prophecies, as we have done in this chapter, builds my faith evermore stronger.

Prophecy is a fascinating and important part of the Word of God, but it is just one part of the Bible, and the entire Book is a miracle! The next chapter, about types and shadows of Christ, is equally interesting and exciting.

Types and Shadows of Christ in the Old Testament

THIS CHAPTER contains tough material, so take what you can and leave the rest. Don't let it throw you.

A Radio Bible Class booklet, *How to Enjoy Your Bible,* defines biblical types and shadows as Old Testament institutions, rituals or historical events which, in addition to the literal meanings, picture some New Testament truth.

I have tried to come up with a good analogy to describe "types and shadows," but only one that was clear enough came to mind. It is still not as clear as I'd like, but it's the best I can do.

We all have had some type of camera and are, therefore, acquainted with pictures and prints. Consequently, we also know that for every picture taken there is a negative. (Please disregard the adverse connotations of the word *negative.*) If we hold a negative up to the light, we can see shadows and shapes. This is vaguely analagous to types and shadows of the Old Testament. The New Testament times of Jesus Christ are the full picture or print in living color!

Hebrews 10:1: "For the law [of the Old Testament], *having a shadow of good things to come and not the very image of the things . . .*" (KJV).

Jesus Christ is the very image of those shadows!

Luke 24:27: "Then Jesus quoted them passage after passage from the writings of the prophets, beginning with the book of Genesis and going right on through the Scriptures, explaining what the passages meant *and what they said about himself.*"

Hebrews 3:5: "Well, Moses did a fine job working in God's house, but he was only a servant; and his work was mostly

to illustrate and suggest those things that would happen
later on."
I hope the fun of looking at the types and shadows will
stimulate you to study deeper and deeper, and also, that it
will help you to see, once again as in the previous section,
the relationship between the Old Testament and the New
Testament. One cannot be complete without the other!

The wilderness journey in Exodus is so rich in types and
shadows of the New Testament that it seems the best
choice to examine in this book. This does not mean that
there are not many more in every book and chapter. There
are probably a few, if not many, on every page in the Bible.
(In the section, "Why Did Jesus Have to Die?" we looked
at a type, or shadow, of Christ in the third chapter of Genesis. Remember the coats of skins?)

The wilderness journey itself is a shadow of the Christian
walk today. It is a study rich in the lessons God taught his
people then, and which he wants us to apply to our lives
today. I urge you to do an in-depth study of the wilderness
journey with an able teacher in the not-too-distant future.
If you don't know of one, ask the Lord in prayer to lead you
to one.

1 Corinthians 10:11: "All these things happened to them [in
the wilderness] as examples—as *object lessons to us*—to
warn us against doing the same things; *they were written down so that we could read about them and learn
from them* in these last days as the world nears its end."
(For this shadow study, we need to refresh our minds
on some of the symbolism in the chapter "Why are the Jews
God's Chosen People?" We learned there that Ishmael was
born of an Egyptian mother and became the father of the
Arab world as we know it today. We also learned that because Ishmael was born out of Abraham's disobedience,
Egypt symbolizes evil and darkness in the Bible.)

Let's begin by taking a look at Moses, who led the children
through the wilderness. Moses himself is a "type of Christ,"
a deliverer. Moses delivered the Israelites out of the hands
of the Egyptians and into the promised land—but not without God's help!

THE TYPE OF CHRIST (MOSES THE DELIVERER):

OT *Exodus 3:8: "I [Moses] have come to deliver them from the Egyptians and to take them out of Egypt into a good land, a large land, a land* 'flowing with milk and honey'—the land where the Canaanites, Hittites, Amorites, Perizzites, Hivites, and Jebusites live."

CHRIST (WHO DELIVERED US FROM DEATH INTO LIFE):

Romans 3:25: "For God sent Christ Jesus to take the punishment for our sins and to end all God's anger against us. He used Christ's blood and our faith as the means of saving us from his wrath. . . ."

The next example is the shadow of Christ in the crossing of the Red Sea—the redemption provided by Christ.

THE SHADOW OF CHRIST:

OT *Exodus 14:21–22:* "Meanwhile, Moses stretched his rod over the sea, and the Lord opened up a path through the sea, with walls of water on each side; and a strong east wind blew all that night, drying the sea bottom. So the people of Israel walked through the sea on dry ground!"

(The Red Sea is the "redemption" sea. Why? Because it is a beautiful picture of Christ's crucifixion, resurrection, and our resultant salvation. The Scripture above says the waters were literally "walled" on both sides of the Israelites. It took a real act of faith on their part to walk through. The Israelites' first steps through those walls of water are a picture of the crucifixion [death] and the coming out on the other side [safe from the Egyptians—evil and death] is a picture of resurrection and salvation.)

CHRIST (THE REDEEMER):

2 Corinthians 1:10: "And He [Jesus] did help us, and saved us from a terrible death; yes, and we expect him to do it again and again."

Once the Israelites had safely crossed the Red Sea, as the Egyptians were in pursuit, the waters engulfed them and they were all killed. This is a shadow of Christ's victory over evil by his death and resurrection and our resulting redemption (our salvation) by crossing over from death to life.

THE SHADOW (VICTORY OVER EVIL):

OT *Exodus 14:27–28:* "Moses did, and the sea returned to normal beneath the morning light. The Egyptians tried to flee, but the Lord drowned them in the sea. The water covered the path and the chariots and horsemen. *And of all the army of Pharaoh that chased after Israel through the sea, none remained alive.*"

JESUS' VICTORY OVER EVIL:

John 11:25–26: "Jesus told her [Martha], 'I am the one who raises the dead and gives them life again. *Anyone who believes in me, even though he dies like anyone else, shall live again. He is given eternal life for believing in me and shall never perish. . . .'*"

Ephesians 2:1: "And you hath he made alive, who were dead in trespasses and sins" (KJV).

Colossians 2:13: "You were dead in sins, and your sinful desires were not yet cut away. Then he gave you a share in the very life of Christ, for he forgave all your sins."

Let's go back over this. The Israelites easily crossed the Red Sea on dry land. After the last of them had crossed over, the walls of the sea collapsed and the Egyptians were swallowed up in it. Thus, God safely delivered the Israelites from the hands of the Egyptians (evil), just as Jesus has done for all who believe in him and claim his redemption, delivering us from our sins (evil) and spiritual death.

Once the Israelites had crossed the Red Sea, the wilderness journey began. Frequently, in the early part of the journey, the Israelites would become extremely impatient with God and his timing (just as Abraham did . . . just as we do today). On such occasions they would complain and gripe about God's way of doing things, railing against him and begging to return to Egypt! A perfect picture of the early Christian walk!

On one such occasion, they murmured (complained) against God (which is a sin, mind you!) because there was no food. Remember there were well over a million people on this journey! . . .

OT   *Exodus 12:37–38:* "That night the people of Israel left Rameses and started for Succoth; *there were six hundred thousand of them, besides all the women and children,* going on foot. People of various sorts went with them; *and there were flocks and herds—a vast exodus of cattle.*" Those 600,000 men, *plus* women, children and other various sorts, *plus* flocks, herds and cattle were making their wilderness journey in what is today known as the Sinai Peninsula. It is still a wilderness, with miles and miles of sand and more sand. There was, therefore, no source of water or food for the multitudes—except the Lord.

Manna was the food God provided.

THE SHADOW:

OT   *Exodus 16:4:* "Then the Lord said to Moses, 'Look, I'm going to rain down food from heaven for them . . .'"

OT   *Exodus 16:14–15:* "And when the dew disappeared later in the morning it left tiny flakes of something as small as hoarfrost on the ground (TLB). And when the children of Israel saw it, they said one to another, It is manna [translates "What is it?"]: for they knew not what it was. And Moses said unto them, This is the bread which the Lord hath given you to eat" (KJV).

CHRIST:

John 6:32–35: "Jesus said, 'Moses didn't give it to them. My Father did. And now he offers you true Bread from heaven. The true Bread is a Person—the one sent by God from heaven, and he gives life to the world.' 'Sir,' they said, 'give us that bread every day of our lives!' Jesus replied, '*I am the Bread of Life.* No one coming to me will

ever be hungry again. Those believing in me will never thirst.'"
(What Jesus is saying here is that once you have accepted him as Lord of your life—to rule supremely in your life— you will no longer seek to fill the void within you. You have filled the void with the only thing which would fill it.)

John 6:48–51: "*Yes, I am the Bread of Life!* When your fathers in the wilderness ate bread from the skies, they all died. But the Bread from heaven gives eternal life to everyone who eats it. *I am that Living Bread that came down out of heaven.* Anyone eating this Bread shall live forever; this Bread is my flesh given to redeem humanity."

The next problem was thirst!

OT   *Exodus 17:3:* "But tormented by thirst, they cried out, 'Why did you ever take us out of Egypt? Why did you bring us here to die, with our children and cattle too?' "

It's not surprising that God had an answer for the problem, is it? In spite of their complaints and rebellious spirits, God provided their needs . . . just as he does for us today.

The SHADOWS (CHRIST, CRUCIFIXION AND THE HOLY SPIRIT):

OT   *Exodus 17:5–6:* "Then Jehovah said to Moses, 'Take the elders of Israel with you and lead the people out to Mt. Horeb. I will meet you there *at the rock. . . .*' "

CHRIST:

OT   *Psalm 18:31:* "For who is God, save the Lord? Or *who is a rock, save our God?*" (KJV).

      1 Corinthians 10:1–4: "For we must never forget, dear brothers, what happened to our people in the wilderness long ago. God guided them by sending a cloud that moved along ahead of them; and he brought them all safely through the waters of the Red Sea. This might be called their 'baptism'—baptized both in sea and cloud!— as followers of Moses [the deliverer]—their commitment to him as a leader. And by a miracle God sent them food to eat and water to drink there in the desert; they drank the water that Christ gave them. He was there with them as a mighty *Rock* of spiritual refreshment."

THE SHADOW (CRUCIFIXION):

OT **Exodus 17:5–6** (*cont.*): " '. . . Strike it with your rod—the same one you struck the Nile with—and water will come pouring out, enough for everyone!' . . ."

CHRIST'S CRUCIFIXION:

OT **Isaiah 53:4:** "Surely he hath borne our griefs, and carried our sorrows; yet *we did esteem him stricken, smitten of God and afflicted*" (KJV).
Mark 15:25: "And it was the third hour; and *they crucified him*" (KJV).

THE SHADOW (THE HOLY SPIRIT):

OT **Exodus 17:5–6** (*cont.*): ". . . Moses did as he was told, and *the water gushed out!*"

THE HOLY SPIRIT:

John 16:7: " 'But the fact of the matter is that it is best for you that I [Jesus] go away, for if I don't, the Comforter [the Holy Spirit] won't come. *If I do, he will—for I will send him to you.*' " [This Scripture quotes Jesus as saying that he must die and be resurrected and ascend into heaven before the Holy Spirit can come.]
John 7:37–39: "On the last day, the climax of the holidays, Jesus shouted to the crowds, 'If anyone is thirsty, let him come to me and drink. For the Scriptures declare that *rivers of living water shall flow from the inmost being of anyone who believes in me.*' " (*He was speaking of the Holy Spirit,* who would be given to everyone believing in him; but the Spirit had not yet been given, because Jesus had not yet returned to his glory in heaven.)
John 4:14: " 'But *the water I give them,*' he said, '*becomes a*

perpetual spring within them, watering them forever with eternal life.'"

Revelation 22:17: " 'The Spirit and the bride say, "Come." Let each one who hears them say the same, "Come." Let the thirsty one come—anyone who wants to; let him come and drink the *Water of Life* without charge.' "

Here in two verses (Exod. 17:5-6) are three shadows! The Rock, who is Jesus Christ; the smiting of the Rock, which is the crucifixion; and the water, who is the Holy Spirit.

These are just seven examples of types and shadows of Christ in the Old Testament; the Bible is full of them. Wouldn't you like to go beyond this study we have done? The Bible is as current and timely for our Christian walk today as it was "in the beginning."

1 Corinthians 10:1-5: "For we must never forget, dear brothers, what happened to our people in the wilderness long ago. God guided them by sending a cloud that moved along ahead of them; and he brought them all safely through the waters of the Red Sea. This might be called their 'baptism'—baptized both in sea and cloud!— as followers of Moses—their commitment to him as their leader. And by a miracle God sent them food to eat and water to drink there in the desert; they drank the water that Christ gave them. He was there with them as a mighty Rock of spiritual refreshment. Yet after all this most of them did not obey God, and he destroyed them in the wilderness."

1 Corinthians 10:11: "All these things happened to them as examples—as object lessons to us—to warn us against doing the same things; they were written down so that we could read about them and learn from them. . . .' "

Through the Word of God he is teaching me. He is teaching me that he is faithful and that I can trust him. The more I trust him, the less I murmur. The less I murmur, the more he reveals of himself to me.

If as you have been reading this book you have allowed the Holy Spirit to teach you, you should by now have a foundation upon which to build a great personal relationship with the Lord. Nothing would delight the Lord more than for you to add more bricks to that foundation . . . but you must be open to his leading!

You have had the hors d'oeuvres. The feast awaits.

My prayer for you . . .

OT *Isaiah 55:11:* "So also is my Word. I send it out and it always produces fruit. *It shall accomplish all I want it to, and prosper everywhere I send it.*"

OT *Psalm 147:18: "He sendeth out his word, and melteth them:* he causeth his wind to blow, and the waters flow" (KJV).

OT *Isaiah 28:10:* "He tells us everything over and over again, a line at a time and in such simple words!"

OT *Isaiah 28:10:* "For precept must be upon precept, precept upon precept; line upon line, line upon line; here a little, and there a little" (KJV).

Ephesians 1:17–22: "I have never stopped thanking God for you. I pray for you constantly, asking God, the glorious Father of our Lord Jesus Christ, to give you wisdom to see clearly and really understand who Christ is and all that he has done for you. I pray that your hearts will be flooded with light so that you can see something of the future he has called you to share. I want you to realize that God has been made rich because we who are Christ's have been given to him! I pray that you will begin to understand how incredibly great his power is to help those who believe him. It is that same mighty power that raised Christ from the dead and seated him in the place of honor at God's right hand in heaven, far, far above any other king or ruler or dictator or leader. Yes, his honor is far more glorious than that of anyone else either in this world or in the world to come. And God has put all things under his feet and made him the supreme Head of the church— which is his body, filled with himself, the Author and Giver of everything everywhere." In Jesus' name. Amen.

TWO LAST THOUGHTS

1. Churchianity vs. Christianity
2. Love One Another
3. P.S.

Churchianity vs. Christianity

THE WORLD IS filled with religious people, many of whom are reaching and stretching up to God to no avail. Through Jesus Christ, God reaches down to all the children of the earth. As long as you are in a Christ-centered church, a church which recognizes the *divinity* of Christ, his death and resurrection, it doesn't matter which church you attend. The principles in this book are not meant to separate you from your church, but rather to enrich your church experience.

I have talked to hundreds of people who were very religious but who never felt as if they "knew" God. They were quietly and secretly frustrated, and many did not know why. To learn that they could really have a personal relationship with him, that he was not some remote "Being" who was unreachable, was immensely thrilling to them.

There are also many people I have met who would defend their "religion" to the death and yet would never speak of Jesus Christ to a soul. But Jesus, rather than buildings or the people and things in them, should be at the core of our worship.

The entire book of Matthew is about religious people who did not know God personally. It should be required reading for every Christian.

Matthew 7:21–23: "Not every one that saith unto me, Lord, Lord, shall enter into the kingdom of heaven, *but he that doeth the will of my Father, who is in heaven.* Many will say to me in that day, Lord, Lord, have we not prophesied in thy name? And in thy name have cast out demons? And in thy name done many wonderful works? *And then will*

I profess unto them, I never knew you; depart from me,
ye that work iniquity" (KJV).
Paul also had a lot to say about having a personal relationship with Jesus Christ.

Acts 17:22–31: "So Paul, standing before them at the Mars
Hill forum, addressed them as follows:

" 'Men of Athens, I notice that you are very religious,
for as I was out walking I saw your many altars, and one
of them had this inscription on it—*"To the Unknown
God." You have been worshiping him without knowing
who he is,* and now I wish to tell you about him.

"He made the world and everything in it, and since he
is Lord of heaven and earth, he doesn't live in man-made
temples; and human hands can't minister to his needs—
for he has no needs! He himself gives life and breath to
everything, and satisfies every need there is. He created
all the people of the world from one man, Adam, and
scattered the nations across the face of the earth. He decided beforehand which should rise and fall, and when.
He determined their boundaries.

"His purpose in all of this is that they should seek after
God, and perhaps feel their way toward him and find him
—though he is not far from any one of us. For in him we
live and move and are! As one of your own poets says it,
"We are the sons of God." If this is true, we shouldn't think
of God as an idol made by men from gold and silver or
chipped from stone. God tolerated man's past ignorance
about these things, but now he commands everyone to
put away idols and worship only him. For he has set a
day for justly judging the world by the man [Jesus] he has
appointed, and has pointed him out by bringing him back
to life again.' "

OT   *Proverbs 16:25:* "There is a way that seemeth right unto a
      man, but the end thereof are the ways of death" (KJV).
God looks upon our hearts, not how many times we go to
church . . . not how much money we give to good causes
. . . not how religious we are.

OT   *Proverbs 21:2:* "Every way of a man is right in his own eyes,
      but the Lord pondereth the hearts" (KJV).

Luke 18:9–14: "Then he [Jesus] told this story to some who
boasted of their virtue and scorned everyone else: 'Two

men went to the Temple to pray. One was a proud, self-righteous Pharisee, and the other a cheating tax collector. The proud Pharisee "prayed" this prayer: "Thank God, I am not a sinner like everyone else, especially like that tax collector over there! For I never cheat, I don't commit adultery, I go without food twice a week [fast], and I give to God a tenth of everything I earn." [Oh, what pride!] But the corrupt tax collector stood at a distance and dared not even lift his eyes to heaven as he prayed, but beat upon his chest in sorrow, exclaiming, "God, be merciful to me, a sinner." I tell you, this sinner, *not* the Pharisee, returned home forgiven! For the proud shall be humbled, but the humble shall be honored.' "

Let him give you a new heart.

OT **Ezekiel 36:26:** "And I will give you a new heart—I will give you new and right desires—and put a new spirit within you. I will take out your stony hearts of sin and give you new hearts of love."

Remember . . . Jesus Christ *is* the church.

1 Corinthians 12:12–13: "Our bodies have many parts, but the many parts make up only one body when they are all put together. *So it is with the 'body' of Christ. Each of us is a part of the one body of Christ.* Some of us are Jews, some are Gentiles, some are slaves and some are free. But the Holy Spirit has fitted us all together into one body. *We have been baptized into Christ's body by the one Spirit,* and have all been given that same Holy Spirit."

Ephesians 1:22–23: "And God has put all things under his feet and made him the supreme Head of *the church—which is his body,* filled with himself, the Author and Giver of everything everywhere."

Colossians 1:18: "*He is the Head of the body made up of his people—that is, his church*—which he began.*"

Enjoy your church home. Enjoy the fellowship, the preaching, and the teaching! Love your minister, pastor, or priest, and the members of your church. But, please, please, please . . . know and love your God above everyone and everything. Know why you are there. Go to worship and learn about *him.*

Matthew 22:37: "Jesus replied, *'Love the Lord your God with all your heart, soul, and mind.' "*

Love One Another

1 Corinthians 13:1–8: "Though I speak with the tongues of men and of angels, and have not love, I am become as sounding bronze, or a tinkling cymbal. And though I have the gift of prophecy, and understand all mysteries, and all knowledge; and though I have all faith, so that I could remove mountains, *and have not love, I am nothing.* And though I bestow all my goods to feed the poor, and though I give my body to be burned, *and have not love, it profiteth me nothing.* Love suffereth long, and is kind; love envieth not; love vaunteth not itself, is not puffed up, doth not behave itself unseemly, seeketh not its own, is not easily provoked, thinketh no evil, rejoiceth not in iniquity, but rejoiceth in the truth; beareth all things, believeth all things, hopeth all things, endureth all things. *Love never faileth. . . ."* (KJV).

There is and always has been much controversy and conflict among believers. Man struggles to accomplish what only God can. One believer struggles to convince another believer that his particular beliefs are the only way. Yet Jesus said *he* was the only way.

John 14:6: "Jesus told him, 'I am the Way—yes, and the Truth and the Life. No one can get to the Father except by means of me.'"

Peter was saved by believing one thing!

Matthew 16:16: "Simon Peter answered, 'The Christ, the Messiah, the Son of the Living God.'"

The thief on the cross was saved by believing one thing!

Luke 23:42: "Then he [the thief] said, 'Jesus, remember me when you come into *your* Kingdom.'"

The entire crux of Christianity rests on *one* fact: *Jesus is Lord!* It is up to the Holy Spirit to take it from there.

Romans 10:9–10: "For if you tell others with your own mouth that Jesus Christ is Lord, and believe in your own heart that God has raised him from the dead, you will be saved. For it is by believing in his heart that a man becomes right with God; and with his mouth he tells others of his faith, confirming his salvation."

Why? Because ". . . no man can say that Jesus is Lord but by the (indwelling) Holy Spirit" (1 Cor. 12:3).

It grieves me to see Christians slugging it out over doctrinal differences. This cannot be glorifying to God! I have seen groups of Christians actually avoid other groups because neither could leave the other free to believe what they believe! Oh, the accusations that fly back and forth! How this must grieve our Lord!

I do not believe God does things this way. This is one area in our Christian lives in which we have given Satan much ground. I have seen evidence of this in my own life, and I repent of this sin and ask God to forgive me and change me, to open up my heart to a deeper faith in his wisdom for all who believe in him. If we trust in him, he will lead us into all truth.

John 16:13: "When the Holy Spirit, who is truth, comes, he shall guide you into all truth. . . ."

James 1:18: "Of his own will *begot he us with the Word of truth,* that we should be a kind of first fruits of his creatures" (KJV).

The Lord understands our human frailties far better than we do. We cannot possibly all be in the "same place at the same time." That is why God leaves us free. I am not saying here that we should not be open to teaching, because we very much need teaching, but the Holy Spirit is the ultimate teacher. The Holy Spirit must be the one to sort through the human teachings and instill in our hearts what is truth, because man cannot possibly know perfect truth.

1 John 2:27: "But you have received the Holy Spirit and he lives within you, in your hearts, so that you don't need anyone to teach you *what is right*. For he teaches you all things, and *he is the Truth*, and no liar; and so, just as he has said, you must live in Christ, never to depart from him."

For myself, I want to hear all Christian viewpoints! Then, the Holy Spirit can plant in my heart that which he wants for me . . . and I have found that he is faithful to do that. At the same time, I am willing to share what I believe and why.

1 Peter 3:15: "Quietly trust yourself to Christ your Lord and if anybody asks you why you believe as you do, be ready to tell him, and do it in a gentle and respectful way."

This Scripture doesn't say anything about cramming your belief down someone's throat. It doesn't say anything about snubbing someone or some group because they don't believe exactly as you do. In fact, Jesus spoke very clearly to this problem. His disciples came running to him concerned about a group of believers who were not following them and their teachings to the letter.

Mark 9:38–42: "One of his disciples, John, told him [Jesus] one day, 'Teacher, we saw a man using your name to cast out demons; but we told him not to, for *he isn't one of our group.*' 'Don't forbid him!' Jesus said. 'For no one doing miracles *in my name* will quickly turn against me. *Anyone who isn't against us is for us.* If anyone so much as gives you a cup of water because you are Christ's—*I say this solemnly*—he won't lose his reward. But if someone causes one of these little ones who believe in me to lose faith—it would be better for that man if a huge millstone were tied around his neck and he were thrown into the sea.'"

That's pretty clear!

I am not saying that we cannot have a discussion with another about our beliefs; but, remember, condemnation does not come from God.

John 3:17: "*God did not send his Son into the world to condemn it, but to save it.*"

Romans 8:1: "So, *there is now no condemnation awaiting those who belong to Christ Jesus.*"

I know many people who profess love for Jesus Christ, yet

who don't seem to believe anything Christian, and as I share my understanding of biblical truth with them I find that there are conflicts. What God has shown me is that they are *his* children, *his* creatures, and the greatest thing I can do for them—and for myself—is, instead of arguing, pray for them (and myself) that God will teach all of us, open us up to *his* truth; and to have unconditional love and acceptance (as much as I am able) for all men, regardless of what we believe, with no strings attached. These matters are really up to him.

The Bible and the guidance of the Holy Spirit should be our guide in all matters. For it is written—

Colossians 1:9: "For this cause we also, since the day we heard it, do not cease to pray for you, and to desire *that ye might be filled with the knowledge of his will in all wisdom and spiritual understanding*" (KJV).

No matter how much knowledge we have about him, without love it means nothing.

1 Corinthians 13:1–3: "Though I speak with the tongues of men and of angels, *and have not love, I am become as sounding bronze, or a tinkling cymbal.* And though I have the gift of prophecy, and understand all mysteries, and all knowledge; and though I have all faith, so that I could remove mountains, *and have not love, I am nothing.* And though I bestow all my goods to feed the poor, and though I give my body to be burned, *and have not love, it profiteth me nothing*" (KJV).

Here we are . . . back where we started.

OT   **Proverbs 21:2:** "Every way of a man is right in his own eyes; but *the Lord pondereth the hearts*" (KJV).

My prayer for you is—

Lord, dear Lord, teach your little ones to be free in what they believe . . . that they may leave others free from condemnation in what they believe. Thank you for telling us in John 8:36 that if the Son sets us free, we will indeed be free. Praise your holy name! In Christ's name, we pray. Amen.

P.S. If this book doesn't sell one copy . . . it has still blessed me. It has taught me beyond words. The book was written out of my love and caring for him which overflows to his creatures, and he has "opened up the windows of heaven for me and poured out a blessing so great I don't have room within me to take it in!" (Mal. 3:10). As I was finishing these last pages, the Holy Spirit revealed to me a miracle which has taken place within me (and without my awareness) over the past weeks and months of writing. He has given me "a new heart and right desires; he has put a new Spirit within me." I was deeply committed to Christ before . . . but I shall never be the same! I feel like Hagar when she said, "I saw God and lived to tell it." For that I thank you for whom it is written. To God goes the glory and all the credit. I was a willing heart, but the Spirit of God has literally poured out his love for his creatures onto these pages, much to my benefit, and I hope, yours.

OT   *Psalm 84:5–7:* "Happy are those who are strong in the Lord, who want above all else to follow your steps. When they walk through the Valley of Weeping it will become a place of springs where pools of blessing and refreshment collect after rains! They will grow constantly in strength and each of them is invited to meet with the Lord in Zion."